Raise Up

8 Owls Publishing creates books that effectively advance God's Kingdom. You may find the full list of books we offer on our website at 8owlspublishing.com.

Copyright © 2023
First Edition

Cover Design: Savanna Holubec
Interior Design: 8 Owls Publishing

All rights reserved. No part of this book may be used or reproduced in any manner whatsoever without written permission from the publisher and copyright holders. Requests should be mailed to 8 Owls Publishing, 111 Windermere St, Waxahachie, Texas, 75165

Please note that 8 Owls Publishing uses capitalization when referencing God and/or other Kingdom terminology that may differ from other publishers or grammatical trends.

ISBN: 978-1-952618-16-1

Scriptures marked (AMP) are taken from the Amplified Bible, Copyright © 2015 by The Lockman Foundation. Used by permission.

Scriptures marked (ESV) are from the ESV® Bible (The Holy Bible, English Standard Version®), © 2001 by Crossway, a publishing ministry of Good News Publishers. Used by permission. All rights reserved. The ESV text may not be quoted in any publication made available to the public by a Creative Commons license. The ESV may not be translated in whole or in part into any other language.

Scriptures marked (KJV) are taken from the Kings James Version.

Scriptures marked (MSG) are taken from THE MESSAGE, copyright © 1993, 2002, 2018 by Eugene H. Peterson. Used by permission of NavPress. All rights reserved. Represented by Tyndale House Publishers.

Scriptures marked (NASB 1995) are taken from the New American Standard Bible ®, Copyright © 1960, 1971, 1977, 1995, 2020 by The Lockman Foundation. All rights reserved.

The "NASB", "NAS," "New American Standard Bible," and "New American Standard," are trademarks registered in the United States Patent and Trademark Office by The Lockman Foundation. Use of these trademarks requires the permission of The Lockman Foundation.

Scriptures marked (NIV) are taken from the Holy Bible, New International Version®, NIV®. Copyright © 1973, 1978, 1984, 2011 by Biblica, Inc.™ Used by permission of Zondervan. All rights reserved worldwide. www.zondervan.com The "NIV" and "New International Version" are trademarks registered in the United States Patent and Trademark Office by Biblica, Inc.™

Scriptures marked (NKJV) taken from the New King James Version®. Copyright © 1982 by Thomas Nelson. Used by permission. All rights reserved.

Scriptures marked (NLT) are taken from the Holy Bible, New Living Translation, copyright © 1996, 2004, 2015 by Tyndale House Foundation. Used by permission of Tyndale House Publishers, Inc., Carol Stream, Illinois 60188. All rights reserved.

Scriptures marked (TPT) are from The Passion Translation ®. Copyright © 2017, 2018, 2020 by Passion & Fire Ministries, Inc. Used by permission. All rights reserved. ThePassionTranslation.com

Table of Contents

Raise Up Lyrics

Introduction

Chapter 1: Heather's Discovery
   God is a Father to the Fatherless 1
Chapter 2: Christy's Journey
   From Grief to Renewal..18
Chapter 3: Kelly's Struggle
   Confronting the Reality of Depression.......................33
Chapter 4: Liz's Story
   Defeating Dysfunction...49
Chapter 5: Bev's Valleys
   Navigating Loss, Lies & Witchcraft...........................65
Chapter 6: Laura Anne's Faith
   Exploring the Depths Beyond the Shallows................83
Chapter 7: Thresa's Redemption
   Overcoming the Unexpected.................................102
Chapter 8: Tammy's Unveiling
   Addressing Generational Sins................................119
Chapter 9: Jessica's Blessing
   Adoption's Path to Multiplying Faith........................135
Chapter 10: Victoria's Transformation
   A Journey from Single to Blended Family.................162
Chapter 11: Sara's Survival
   Confronting Abuse and Reclaiming Life...................169
Chapter 12: Shelsea's Exodus
   Escaping Egypt's Hold and Finding Freedom............187

Write Your Story

About The Authors

Raise Up ©

Lyrics By: Victoria Steelman, Shellem Cline, Shelsea Becker

(Verse 1)
*Woke up this morning
I felt it again
God is a planning
A great awakening
The spirit of Him who raised Jesus from the dead
Is living in you just like the Bible saide*

(Chorus)
*It's time to RAISE UP!
Women of God
Taking on the devil
Every mile that we trod
It's time to RAISE UP!
And set the standard
Marching on and waving
Our victory banner
RAISE UP!
SHE WILL RAISE UP!*

(Verse 2)
*Working together
One mind and accord
Growing the Kingdom
Of our risen Lord
Learning and leaning, filling your cup
Hear the voice of Jesus saying, "WARRIORS GET UP!"*

CHORUS

RAISE UP!
SHE WILL RAISE UP!

(Bridge)
RAISE UP all you believers
RAISE UP mighty women of God
RAISE UP the standard of leaders
RAISE UP mighty women of God
(x2)

CHORUS

RAISE UP!
SHE WILL RAISE UP!
RAISE UP!

Introduction

We invite you to embark on a "Raise Up" journey through the heartfelt and inspiring personal stories from the women on our team here at She Will Conference. Each narrative vividly captures the intimate relationship between God and His people. In this captivating collection of God stories, you'll witness how these personal encounters with the Holy Spirit have shaped lives, families, and even the world around us.

In the pages that follow, you'll discover a tapestry of intimately personal stories – each a unique thread woven into the rich fabric of human experience. As you read through these narratives, we invite you to not only connect with the storytellers but to embark on your own RAISE UP story.

At the end of each chapter lies a set of questions that delve deep into the emotions, choices, and moments that have defined these stories. These questions are not mere prompts; they are your keys to unlocking your own memories, reflections, and insights. As you read, pause and ponder. Allow the stories to act as mirrors, reflecting back the chapters of your own life.

But this collection is not simply meant to be read and set aside. It's an interactive invitation – an opportunity for you to become both reader and author. By engaging with the questions provided, you'll gradually piece together your own narrative. By the time you finish this book, you'll have crafted your own testimonial story, a testament to your unique journey.

We encourage you to take the insights you've gathered, the emotions you've felt, and the realizations you've uncovered, and put them into words. Share your story with the She Will team, because we believe that your experiences have the potential to inspire, uplift, and connect. Your journey is a part of this collection, and your voice deserves to be heard.

Thank you for allowing these stories to become a part of your own narrative. As you read, reflect, and write, remember that your story is a source of strength – not just for you, but for all those who will be touched by your words. Embrace this opportunity, and let your RAISE UP story help build other's faith.

> *"And they overcame him by the blood of the Lamb and by the word of their testimony, and they did not love their lives to the death."*
> Revelation 12:11 NKJV

Please submit your RAISE UP story to: yourstory@lynministries.org

With anticipation,
~Shelsea

We couldn't write a story of how God moved and worked in our lives without first asking: Do you know Him? Is Jesus your personal Savior? If so, then as you read this book, we hope you are encouraged that you are not alone and find hope in Him that no matter your situation, circumstances, or hand of life that was dealt, He can redeem, save, and find worthy even your darkest places.

If you do not know Him or are unsure, Romans 10:10 says, "For it is with your heart that you believe and are justified, and it is with your mouth that you profess your faith and are saved." (NIV) Salvation is simple: Jesus, come into my heart and help me to walk in Your footsteps daily. I believe that only You can save me, and I want access to the Living Water that You give.

Amen! We encourage you to find Him, find a church or people who believe, open the Word, and speak: "God help!" He will be faithful to answer!

~Heather

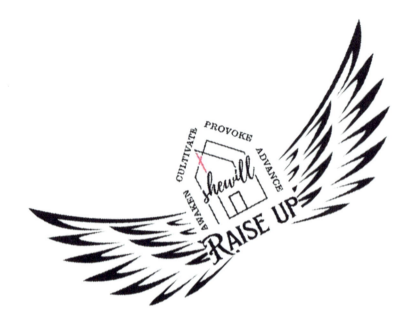

Chapter One
Heather Grissom

… HEATHER GRISSOM

Heather's Discovery:
God Is A Father To The Fatherless

    I know God as many things; Healer, Provider, Gracious, Patient, Loving, Gentle, Forgiving, and so much more, but what I know Him best as is a Father to the fatherless. This is a testament of how the Father took an orphan and raised her up to be a warrior.

    First of all, my name is Heather Grissom. I am a West Texas-born girl who married my high school sweetheart, with 3 beautiful children and a heart of worship. My husband is a pastor in Southeast Missouri and we've served the local church faithfully for 17 years. This is not the life I thought I would have when I was young and dreaming, but God has faithfully surpassed all my wildest dreams and proven faithful to walk with me through every step. God has proven over and over throughout my life that the calling that He placed on me has the final say, that light always overcomes darkness, and that when the enemy thought that he had me, Jesus war cried over me: SHE IS MINE! When you relate to aspects of my testimony, I hope you are encouraged that you are not alone, you find hope that God's hand is always working, and that it points you closer to Jesus!

    Let's start at the beginning; I was not born into a Godly family. I did not grow up in church, learning about God, reading the Bible, and singing VBS songs. I grew up very poor with a mother who didn't know how to be a mother. My sister and I learned to ride out the highs and the lows and the manipulation and being left totally alone for days, oftentimes without food or electricity. On the outside, we would play the part when she was in a good mood and try to pretend like the darkness wasn't there. I would hold on to the good moments like my life depended on it, because to be honest, it did. I turned myself into the perfect, straight-A child who would keep the house immaculate so maybe she

RAISE UP

would stay this time. I learned to care for my sister and guard her against as much of the ugly as I possibly could. It was a weight I was never meant to bear, but God had a plan for me, and even in those lonely and scary moments, He was holding me. Joshua 1:9 (ESV) says, *"Have I not commanded you? Be strong and courageous. Do not be frightened, and do not be dismayed, for the LORD your God is with you wherever you go."* As a young child, I did not know this verse. I didn't have it yet to speak when I was afraid. But it's just like our Father to know the plans that He has for us and give His children a hand of protection because He is truly with us wherever we go.

    Throw into the mix a retired marine stepfather who was an alcoholic, pathological liar, and liked to use me as a punching bag at the slightest inconvenience. I was born into a generational curse of darkness and doomed to repeat a life of addiction, abuse, violence, and selfishness…….but GOD. God saw this abused, neglected, and damaged child and spoke life into me. God knew that His plan for me was to break this curse and step into the light. His hand was raising me up to be a warrior, but He still had to do some cultivating to get me there. I still had years of protection and guidance to come, and this was only the beginning. I spent years being the beaten and neglected girl, trying with all of her might to protect her sister and lie to hide the truth of what was happening at home. I spent years taking the blame for their anger as if it were my fault. I spent years thinking that this was normal and I was just unlucky.

    Then I turned 15, and it all took a turn for the worse, or so I thought. That year set into motion God's plans of redemption for the life I lived and set ablaze a stirring inside my heart to know who He was. My mother was divorced by my stepfather that year, which seemed like a breath of air, but was short-lived. She walked away from my life and into the arms of a boyfriend right after my 16th birthday. The abused and neglected little girl was now an orphan. I had begun to label myself as unwanted, unworthy of love, and in desperate need of something to fill in the broken pieces. But God had been faithful to protect me this far. I was still alive, and redemption was on the way.

    God placed a high school coach into my life to pour Jesus' love onto me through kindness, love, and basketball. I know she saw the hurt and that no one ever showed up for a game, but she didn't see something unworthy. Coach Val was placed into my life by God's own hand to make me strong, read scripture over me and the team, and invite us into a loving, God-filled home. That home was a place of refuge for two years of high school and was the first place that I could look back in hindsight and see how God had placed a person on my path to speak life into me and start to point me to Him.

About that same time, God threw my future husband into my life. He came in like a wrecking ball of loving Jesus and unashamed pursuit of the Father. If I'm being honest, he terrified me and intrigued me, and made me feel ashamed of who I was. But God! He had a plan! Jeremiah 29:11-14 (NIV) was just starting to come together in a tangible way that I would see:

"For I know the plans I have for you," declares the Lord, "plans to prosper you and not to harm you, plans to give you hope and a future. Then you will call on me and come and pray to me, and I will listen to you. You will seek me and find me when you seek me with all your heart. I will be found by you," declares the Lord, "and will bring you back from captivity."

I spent the remainder of my high school years serving in youth church with my boyfriend, playing every sport available, and killing myself to get every good grade and every scholarship possible to get me as far away from West Texas as humanly possible. I survived that, I graduated, my boyfriend's family embraced me and loved me like their own, I worked a great full-time job on the side of school and everything else to provide for my sister and myself, and I was planning my life, within my own strength, to escape. But the thing with moving in your own strength is you get in your own way, and you can't sustain it. Isaiah 40:29 (NIV) says, *"He gives strength to the weary and increases the power of the weak."* This scripture is so true and comes into play down the road, but at that moment, I didn't understand Him. I was playing church with my boyfriend and having a constant battle in my mind between who the scripture was teaching me He is and who I am and what my past had already defined me as. The devil started seeing the calling that God was placing on my life and threw me for a curve ball. I

RAISE UP

tore my knee up my senior year of basketball and that was my fast-track ticket far, far away. Now what?

I graduated, let my steady God-loving boyfriend move away, and I started at a junior college twenty miles from where I grew up. I went to the darkest place during that time. I felt more alone than I ever had, and my mother showed up again after years of being away, with a newer boyfriend and increased manipulation. I let her pull me back into her darkness, let her addictions and pain spread into my heart. I felt trapped again. There was not a glimmer of hope waiting, and I let the darkness overtake the light until November.

I got to see my long-distance boyfriend who was thriving at a Christian college, growing in his walk with the Lord, and still serving in church and finding himself and the calling that God had placed on his life. I was so jealous of the light that was within him. I wanted to know this hope and freedom. I wanted to know this love that he knew. I wanted to be anywhere but where I was. I questioned how God could love him and not want me. I questioned who He was, why me, why this life, where was He when the church said He is supposed to defend and protect, where was He my whole life? This moment of all consuming brokenness is the first moment in my life that I felt like God spoke to me. I wish I could say that I heard it in this loud booming voice that told me exactly what to do and how the story would end, but that's just not how He works, and the older I get, the more I'm thankful for that character aspect of His. I felt in that moment of desperation that God was telling me, "I've never left you sweet girl; you just don't know Me yet. Come know Me!" So the very next day, I enrolled into the Christian college with my then-boyfriend, left everything within the next few weeks, and moved to Brownwood to go to school. Within a year, my boyfriend became my fiancé, and we were married that summer. I had finally escaped! That's it, the end. I got saved, I got married, and life became peachy. Did you chuckle? Yeah, so did I as I wrote it because we know salvation isn't a punch ticket to easy and happy, and marriage isn't an escape and didn't fix the orphan who was broken and lonely. But this was just the beginning of my story, and the healing that was still to come. The foundation was created in the beginning.

Hope is defined as a feeling of expectation and desire for a certain thing to happen, but scripture defines hope more deeply, *"For in this hope we were saved. But hope that is seen is no hope at all. Who hopes for what they already have?"* (Romans 8:24, NIV) *and "May the God of hope fill you with all joy and peace as you trust in him, so that you may overflow with hope by the power of the Holy Spirit."* (Romans 15:13, NIV). This journey of my life was about to be awakened by the God of hope. God was stirring up a deep well within my soul, but He started with restoring my hope. God had prepared for me a gentle and God-loving man to marry and put me in the path of two more important people: our college pastor and our children's pastor of the church where my husband served as the youth pastor.

    The two years we spent at that church and with those pastors is where the raising up of my dry bones took place. The children's pastor took me in as her own family; her kids loved me, her husband called me his own daughter, and we spent almost every dinner together. They taught me how a family loves and began to help heal the orphaned heart. The more they knew my story, the more they drew me close and for the first time, I got to experience a family void of abuse and full of love. I pushed them away at times because it felt too good, it hurt to feel hope and love, but they kept on pursuing me. They kept choosing me like the Father does to us. Like Luke 15:3-7, I was the lost sheep that kept wandering but kept being pursued.

    Our college pastor at the time also saw in me a gift of worship. The number of unrelenting times that he spoke this over me and gently nudged me closer to the Father were so countless that honestly, without God's strength and intervention, he should have given up on me. But he wasn't working on his own strength and God had told him that I was worth the investment. We started doing a study in Ephesians at our college night, and I left one of the nights with Ephesians 4:1-2 (NIV) ringing in my ears. *"...I urge you to live a life worthy of the calling you have received. Be completely humble and gentle; be patient, bearing with one another in love."* I was not living a life worthy of my calling because, let me be honest, I had no idea what it was. I didn't even know how to ask. So I asked my poor college pastor all the questions. Not just a few, all the questions. And after a lot of time, a lot of patience, and a mountain of reluctance, I agreed to help sing on the college worship team with my husband and some of our friends. This was the first step in

RAISE UP

offering God my gift and over the next year, I encountered the God that did miracles. I encountered moments of clarity on who God was, and began healing a few parts that I was willing to let go of. I experienced God at those college nights in a way that was more than just a feeling in a moment, but something that sustained me throughout the week. I spent months trying to heal that hurt little girl through a Father that was teaching me that He loved me and cared for me.

    I felt like Eve in the garden in Genesis when He asked, *"Who told you that you were naked?"* (Genesis 3:11a, NIV) I kept hearing Him speak over me, "Who told you that you were an orphan? Who told you that you weren't worthy? Who told you that you were alone? Who told you that you didn't matter?" The enemy had held my thoughts captive for twenty years and thought that he had me, but Jesus declared over me, "SHE IS MINE! She is no longer dry bones." I was living Ezekiel 37:5 (NIV), *"This is what the Sovereign Lord says to these bones: I will make breath enter you, and you will come to life."* I was feeling stronger, more secure, and confident to be used. I was healing daily and ready to see God move in a greater way.

    The devil hated this victory; he was terrified of what would happen when I started believing what God was speaking over me and started walking into what He was calling me to be. So he snuck in and let man destroy the church that we were in and stripped me of the family that I had grown to love. His deception spread back into my mind: people will hurt you, you are back to being an orphan, you are back to a state of being unwanted…. BUT GOD. He had a plan and it still included me. He wasn't done teaching me who I was and who He was and was just starting to cultivate the seeds that His faithful servants had planted in my heart.

    We took a youth/worship pastor position in Arkansas and moved far away from any friends or family that we knew. We were following my husband's calling and for a few years, it was easy. We were still newlyweds and enjoying learning each other, the church seemed good, and we had made some friends. I still kept them at a distance because parts of me were not healed yet, but God was using my gift and teaching me what worship truly was. I dug into scripture, not as much as I should have, but more than I ever had before. I wanted this gift to be used for

His glory or I didn't want it. I wanted worship to mean so much more than just music or the opening act of the service on Sunday, and I was finding those answers in the Word and in times of prayer to Him. I was learning my identity in Him:

I am redeemed (Ephesians 1:17).
I am perfectly loved (Ephesians 2).
I am a child of God (1 John 3:1).
I am forgiven (1 John 1:9).
I am fearfully and wonderfully made (Psalm 139:14).
I am never alone (Romans 8:38-39).
I am a new creation (2 Corinthians 5:17).
I am victorious (1 Corinthians 15:57).

In worship, I started to learn to worship Him in all things and to bring the oil to the Sunday service instead of just waiting for the oil to pour out. This time felt peaceful and oddly restful, but then we decided that we needed to expand our family. And with those prayers of joy to expand our family came what felt like an eternity of "not yet" answers to those prayers. It took us over a year to finally read a positive test. During that time, the wait was brutal and I honestly began to understand what faith actually was and that God was not some genie in a bottle just waiting to answer yes to His faithful servants.

I wrestled with the joy of pending motherhood. It brought much fear and anxiety that since I didn't have an example of a good mother, I would epically fail, and that I would somehow repeat the sins of my mother because I was her child. I felt like I didn't deserve this baby and that maybe God made me wait so long because I wasn't worthy. None of this was true. He had released me from these feelings of inadequacy. Romans 13:14 tells us we are clothed with Christ himself, which means we are forever wrapped in his loving arms of grace. He will never leave us wallowing in shame. He clothes us with worth, value, and honor.

Fast forward a few months and He fulfilled His promise to break the generational curse in my life. He gave me my first daughter, and I've never known a joy like I felt having her. Watching my husband be a father began to help heal the word "father" as a bad word in my life. He was not abusive; he was gentle. He was not condemning; he was encouraging. He was not angry; he was patient. He was not hateful; he was loving.

RAISE UP

And the list went on and on. Seeing him father someone that I loved, helped shift my understanding of God the Father, and it opened my eyes to a new level of the character of God. I got to move from the kid table to the adult table. He was more than just an unseen figure that kept my moral compass from doing bad things; He was a Father who cared for His child. My heart was healing. The orphan and unwanted child was letting God fill those empty holes with Him. I became adopted and wanted and I finally began to feel that breath of life that was breathed into my dry bones. God had let me rest and filled my soul with His bread of life, and my strength was renewing. But just like before, the devil knew that I was growing as a threat, and man stepped in, the church hurt us, and we were faced with moving again.

    This is the part of the story where I wish I could write myself into this "religious light" that would make it seem like I had come so far, and I held onto hope, and in the moment could feel God moving me like a beautiful waltz into my next assignment of growth or spiritual enlightenment. That's not what happened next, though. I convinced myself that the churches that hurt me were not people, but they were God, and though I had known Him as faithful and true, and served Him whole-heartedly for years at this point, that I was now on my own and He had left me. I even went as bold as to pray that my husband would leave ministry and that I would never sing another song in a church ever again. I built the walls around my heart so thick that they were impenetrable, and God let me sit there. Not alone, but sitting. I sat there for months. I found out I was pregnant again at the worst time ever; my husband had no job, and hope seemed lost.

    Thankfully, God did not answer my selfish prayers for Patrick to quit ministry, but instead, He answered my husband's faithfulness with a new pastor position further north. We were set to move and were traveling to Texas to celebrate my spiritual sister's wedding, and yet there was no joy to be found in my heart. And then I started to miscarry and my heart shattered into a billion pieces. I became overwhelmed with guilt and grief that God had taken something from me. That He was such a brutal, horrible, God, that in my cries of pain and hurt and mistiming, those were the prayers He heard and answered. He took the only glimmer of light that I had left in the darkness. But in those cries of pain, I served a God who is strong enough to bear the weight of the emotions that I felt. He did not turn away from me, even when I yelled and screamed and punched at him. He was proving that He was the Father I knew Him to be and that I was safe with Him. That in His arms, I would find healing. And even though I was pushing everyone away and turning my heart into stone, that He still found me worthy, and the calling on my life was not done.

He then took 2-3 very painful years to walk me through healing. He healed my trauma. He healed my marriage. He helped me remember my old coach who faithfully walked through miscarriages and clung to the Father and my old college pastors who walked through a miscarriage and clung to God for hope and direction. So I left the seeds of faith and hope to cultivate in my soul for those years, and God began to take the broken pieces from a created foundation to pillars of support. Leviticus 25:3-4 (NIV) was my walk with the Lord: *"For six years sow your fields, and for six years prune your vineyards and gather their crops. But in the seventh year the land is to have a year of sabbath rest, a sabbath to the Lord. Do not sow your fields or prune your vineyards."* I was married in 2006, and until 2013, God was sowing into me and pruning. Then, in 2013, He let me heal and rest. He took the evil and the bad and set in motion His plan to rectify my circumstances for His glory.

This next part is my favorite part of my testimony, this is the part where I started to see my life through the lens of Jesus, and let me tell you, it's a game changer. This is the part where God told His child, the one He had breathed the breath of life into, to finally come alive!! This is the story of the adopted child who becomes a warrior!

Over the next 5 years, God would take my talent, help me multiply it and then use it as a gift for His Kingdom. I would have another daughter to add to our mix, our church would grow, and we would see so much fruit in the seeds that He was using us to sow. We would see hundreds of people come to Jesus and be baptized and life would feel great. My marriage would get stronger daily, my faith in Jesus would grow, and God was using this precious time to fully awaken the calling on my life and help me understand it. He was going to take all the pain and help me see where He would use it for good. I had spent all these years of my life wandering through the wilderness, but what I hadn't seen before was, just like Jesus in Matthew 4:1-11, I wasn't wandering alone.

RAISE UP

And though I was uncomfortable and lonely and in pain, I wasn't walking alone. God was teaching me to pray, He was showing me resilience and He was protecting me.

I was running face-first into my calling to shepherd and lead worship, not just music. God was shaping me into a warrior, and ironically, He was teaching me what He meant every time He said "send Judah first." Judges 1:1-2 and 20:18 depict what is happening in Israel: they are going to war with the Canaanites and the Lord tells them when they are scared and don't know what to do, "send Judah first." Judah, in Hebrew, means praise. So studying this began to awaken the worship leader inside of me. God was digging my roots deeper into Him and helping me see within myself what He had seen all along. He called me to worship because the heartache and hurt and pain had made me strong, made me brave, and made me fearless. It made me see others' pain because I knew what pain looked like. It made me understand the true meaning of beauty from ashes. He had turned the pain into purpose and wanted to awaken the warrior within me. God could send me first into battle, which he does every single Sunday morning, because He knows I will battle, because when He proclaimed *"So do not fear, for I am with you,"* (Isaiah 41:10a, NIV) I would believe it because I lived it. Praise is how I fight; my weapon is the scriptures, prayers, and melodies that I've offered to Him daily, in joy and in pain.

I believe that our worship breaks through things and opens up the deepest parts of ourselves that we try to pretend aren't there. What I have to offer is that I'll battle on your behalf. In fact, as you are reading this, I may not know your name, but I'm praying for you. I'm singing worship over you and fighting with all of Heaven on your behalf for your breakthrough and your redemption. Holy, Holy, Holy is the Lord God Almighty, who was and is and is to come! This is how I fight battles: eyes up, knees to the ground. It starts with worship.

The devil had tried his hardest to keep me from seeing who God saw me as, because I was learning to walk in the authority given to me as a child of the Most High King! In Acts 19:11-20, the seven sons of Sceva lacked the authority to cast the demons out, and the demons laughed, saying *"Jesus I know, and Paul I recognize, but who are you?"* (v.15, ESV) Well, hell knows my name because I am known by the Father,

HEATHER GRISSOM

I commune with him daily, and there is authority when I speak the name of Jesus! Jesus provoked what was always inside of me and can do the same for you! This calling of worship has put me in the line of fire more times than I can count and pushed the limits of my faith, but with my whole heart, I choose Jesus. I choose Kingdom over comfort, and the time spent in these years of growth, healing, and maturing of my faith led me to the journey that was ahead for the last few years! These years made me thankful that I have a testimony to give and gave me the opportunity to reflect and see God's hand on my life.

Beginning in 2019, God was continuing to shape my gift of leading worship but was also cultivating a gift of discernment. He was using the trauma that I had experienced as a child and the people-reading skills that I had painstakingly learned to use for my safety, as a gift to see others. He was using little moments of seeing the pain in someone's eyes through their "I'm doing great," and granting me boldness to say, "Can I pray for you?" The more faithful I was to say yes, the more he opened my eyes to see people through His eyes, and the more I prayed and prayed for others, the more people He sent my way. Luke 16:10 says if you are faithful in the little things, you will be faithful in the big things. This year in my life was the most empowering and yet the most vulnerable.

It also led me to see when our anointing in our current church, the one that had been a shelter for healing, was being lifted. But this time, instead of seeing the church as something to hurt us and feeling the change as an attack on me, I was learning to see it as a preparation for our next assignment. It hurt; I can't tell you that it didn't. We had people who were "family" turn their backs on us and write us out of their lives because we didn't attend the same church anymore. We had people that we sacrificed so much for, say and do the most painful things to us.... but GOD. He knew I had been here before, in the realm of church hurt, but I was different now. I was no longer just bones lying in a desolate desert. I carried the breath of life within me; I was fully raised to life and walking in His calling of my life! I didn't just know who God was, I knew Him intimately, I knew His character, and I was prepared to face what was ahead.

I saw the year of COVID how the devil overtook people with fear. I saw how churches were dying and people were hopeless. I think 2020

RAISE UP

was a pretty dark year for all of us, but as Psalm 34:17 (NIV) tells us, *"The righteous cry out, and the Lord hears them; he delivers them from all their troubles."* Not a single one of us walked alone during that time and God's still turning all things around for His glory. My story is no different. We left our church home of 9 years that year. I felt like I lost my spiritual family that year because of that church and the choices of man. It even took away some of the closest family I had known and changed our relationship into something I didn't recognize, but still, God had a plan for redemption and purpose, and I was ready.

    We spent the next 2 years being hurt over and over by people we loved and trusted. We spent hours in prayer, begging God to tell us what was next, and praying that the loneliness and pain would subside. We spent 2 years searching for our church home and trying to decipher where He was leading us. Can I encourage you if you are walking through the prayers of a "not yet" answer by God, to not lose hope? When money is tight and you don't know how you'll eat, when family walks away from you because it's hard and you're hurt or they're hurt and you feel alone, when friends don't care about you unless you can give them something, and when you are staring in the face of the wait and you are tempted to just muscle your way into an answer; wait! Exodus 14:14 (NIV) says, *"The Lord will fight for you, you need only to be still."* I had to come to a place where I walked out my faith in the wait. It's not faith until it's uncomfortable, right?

    I clung to Daniel 3:18 in what I thought was a no. God was behind the scenes preparing the soil and writing my new chapter. He was still redeeming my story and my family's story; I just had to trust that the Master knew the way. It's easier said than done, but He has proven faithful. I was in a season of preparing again. It was lonely and my emotions often told me it was impossible, but God was removing and He was adding. It was people, and it was habits, and it was things. I couldn't expect this next chapter to look like it had before. Every chapter before had taught me that I had to leave some things behind because everything couldn't go with me. I'd witnessed His faithfulness and seen Him breathe life within! I'd pour out praise to Him. Remember, I'm Judah, send me first!

HEATHER GRISSOM

Now I'm here, in this place, hundreds of miles from anything I've ever known. I'm meeting all new people and figuring out life here in Missouri as a pastor's wife. I'm learning a new community and opening my heart to let them see Jesus in me. I'm still waking up every morning with a song in my heart and a calling to worship Him, a never-ending work in progress, still in desperate need of a Savior! I still stumble and yet He still picks me up, over and over! I am no longer the orphan, but an adopted child. God proved over and over that His promise to be a father to the fatherless was true. He still finds me worthy, and the beauty about adoption into His family is that the blood Jesus shed on the cross covers me in entirety! My story of being raised up will have more chapters, and thank God I will still be able to testify of His faithfulness in them!

RAISE UP

Reflect and Write Your Story
God Is A Father To The Fatherless

Reflect:

In what way does the personal story you've just read connect with your own experiences? Is there common ground between you and the author? Explore the emotions you felt while reading. Where do those feelings stem from and how are they connected to your personal story?

HEATHER GRISSOM

Writing Prompt:

How does the opening of your testimony unfold? Describe the setting, time, location, sensory details like scents and sounds, your age, and the people involved.

RAISE UP

Scripture Connection:

Looking back, can you see where God was in this part of your story? Do any scriptures come to mind?

Chapter Two
Christy Catlin

Christy's Journey:
From Grief To Renewal

This year makes nearly 20 years my husband and I have been in full time ministry together. We have served over the years as associate youth pastors, worship pastors, children's pastors, associate pastors and now, for the last 3 years, we have become the lead pastors of a church plant in the hill country. We see our life's calling as if we enlisted in the military and when God gives us our assignments, we go. This is not an easy life and yet, the empowerment of the Lord to face new challenges and the life-giving presence of the Holy Spirit allows us to face each day with a certainty I would have never known possible in my earlier years. So as a pretty important book once began, let me do the same.

I accepted the Lord at 12 years old and experienced the baptism of the Holy Spirit the very night I met Jesus. This made a profound impact on how I perceived the Lord. It astounded me as I had never stepped foot in a church before and the idea of a Holy Spirit was completely foreign to me. I didn't grow up in church, and my family came to Jesus in the most unorthodox of ways, so I had no background or frame of reference for who the Holy Spirit was but the encounter I experienced forever impacted my life and I still look to it today as a marker in my journey with the Lord.

Unfortunately, my teen years were marked with high highs and low lows as I learned the truth in the statement, "just because you were filled once doesn't mean you stay full". I struggled with faith and consistency and it led me to live a very roller coaster version of Christianity in which I fell often. Riddled with guilt and condemnation, I would struggle to recover and pull myself up again. My early experience with the Holy Spirit was a constant reminder that God had something for me but I didn't maintain an open conversation with him that would allow me access to the power of his spirit in my everyday life. The Holy Spirit was a great accessory to my Christianity but I had yet to understand it as a necessity.

This all culminated in my striving to live out BIG faith essentially in my own strength. At 16 I responded to a call to serve the Lord in ministry with my life and I knew with all my soul that it was my life's purpose. Shortly after, I met a boy who shared that call and served in music ministry at his church while I served as youth pastor of my small church. We dated for 3 years, fell in love and got engaged our freshman year of college. Our plan was to serve the Lord in music ministry and I knew I had finally figured my life out. Life had settled a bit. The roller coaster had eased because my relationship made me steady. **Please catch that!**

I write this now with brilliantly clear hindsight and yet the mere memory of this season brings me right back to the edge of my heartbreak. I had no idea how much trust and identity I had put in my relationship and not in the Lord. I had no grasp of the Holy Spirit's true role in my life as I had all the comfort and companionship I needed in my earthly protector. Thankfully my story isn't one of betrayal, but the lessons I learned took my heart to depths of despair I had never known.

I had traveled out of town to help a church friend and awoke to a missed call from my dad. I returned the call and immediately knew something was wrong just through the tone in which he answered the phone. He only had to say a few words and my whole world collapsed. "Baby, he passed away last night tragically. You should get home, his momma's going to need you." I don't remember much after that except getting in my car and driving 3 hours in silence as I wept with more questions than answers. I survived the calls, texts and people stopping by and endured the funeral in a fog of grief. It wasn't until nearly two weeks later that I faced the realization that I didn't just lose my relationship. I lost my entire future. Every hope, plan and dream was tied up in the promise of serving together. TOGETHER! I was never prepared to serve ALONE!

As the stages of grief naturally progressed, I landed smack dab in the center of anger and parked. I couldn't believe it honestly. Didn't God call me to ministry? Didn't God bring him to me? The perfect one who fit all the criteria and had the same heart? Why would he do that just to take

RAISE UP

him away? Why would he promise me the moon just to steal the sun and the stars too?

Unfortunately, the happiness and security my relationship had given me had taken the place of any real relationship with God somewhere along the way. I had formed my idea of God around the promise of a great life if I served him. I do for you and you do for me. I still had claimed to love God. I still was planning to serve God but somehow my relationship with God must have just been for safety and security and once that was replaced in a physical way, I just needed the guy in the sky for the big stuff and to check in every once in a while.

Instead of curling up at the feet of Jesus and allowing the Holy Spirit to do what he does best, I rejected him altogether, re-boarded the roller coaster and entered the darkest year of my life. It all began with "The List."

"The List" began as a coping tool I had seen somewhere to try to get out of the funk that comes with grief. Instead of using it to cope with pain and plan for the future I used it to list out all the ways I could hurt God for how badly he had hurt me. While I don't believe it is good theology now, a youth pastor growing up had used the analogy of sinning as nailing the nails in Jesus' hands once again and I was so angry that I wrote that list with the intention of causing Jesus pain. I listed out horrible things. Things Christians would never do. Things my friends and family would blush and weep over. I set my intent on crossing every one of them off "The List." I began traveling to friends' apartments on college campuses and partying every weekend. Working crazy hours and sleeping at random places. I spent so many days and weeks lost in a blur of pain it was as if I was in a trance. Until my decisions awoke me to the consequences nearly a year later.

Now, I should let you know that no one knew my plan or my lifestyle. I couldn't deal with the world knowing my pain or my brokenness so I moved away from those close to me and pretended with every phone call that I was doing great. I had a steady, well-paying job and a new home church, which they didn't need to know I had never attended. Yet brokenness does not remain hidden for too long before it reveals itself.

When I awoke in the apartment of someone whose face I didn't even recognize as I left, I felt the earth shift. Something was off. I had come off of a couple week long drunken spree and didn't know what town I was in or where my car was. I threw up in the parking lot of a Kroger, outside a dumpy apartment complex, while I called an old friend to come find me. I was shaking horribly by the time she arrived and, on the drive home, I began bleeding profusely. She panicked and, against my wishes, she drove me to the emergency room and essentially kicked me out of the car and told me to call her when I got my stuff together.

    I limped into the hospital and checked myself in alone. They proceeded to run all the tests and told me I had been 3-5 weeks pregnant and had a miscarriage. My blood alcohol level was through the roof and I remember reading my chart after the doctors and nurses left the room and reading "fetal alcohol poisoning" as cause of death on the record. My stomach twisted at the realization that not only had I had no idea I had been pregnant, but I had no idea by whom. The thought of the death being entirely my fault stunned me and I shut down completely. I was released and had to take a taxi home because I still didn't know where I had left my car and I couldn't bear to call anyone who might want to know what happened.

    I walked into my apartment not knowing how to process everything that was happening. Most profoundly, I felt the most alone I had ever truly felt. Not because I was physically alone, but because not one person in the world knew what I was going through and I didn't even believe anyone would care. I assumed if they did, they would have intervened. I collapsed in a puddle of my own tears and pain and spent hours contemplating if this life was even worth living anymore.

    It was in that thought that something flashed in my memory. I wondered when I had last felt safe and loved. When had I last felt happy? Was this "List" doing any damage to God or was it just doing damage to me? I reached for the flash of memory, that flash of light in my darkness and in that moment, I didn't see a memory of my fiancé which shocked me. I saw a memory of church summer camp where I laid on the floor praying and singing in the presence of the Lord. I saw myself glowing in the radiance of the Holy Spirit and I was perfectly happy, and my fiancé was nowhere around. He had not even entered the picture yet. I sat up suddenly and as I pulled myself together, I realized that the last place I could remember happiness was in church. Maybe God had hurt me but the church had been my safe place. If I could just get to a church maybe

RAISE UP

I could feel happy again. I jumped up and ran to my computer to Google search the nearest church and one of the first search results was a church only a couple miles away and the pastor's name and photo seemed familiar so I took note of their service times for the following Wednesday night and made plans to go.

I walked into the church freshly showered and put together, my Bible under my arm like any good church girl would. I didn't want to stick out or attract attention. I just wanted to sit in the back and feel good again. I didn't go with the intention of making peace with God. I went selfishly to find some reminder of my past life. Of the person I once was who had everything in the world to live for. Yet even in my selfishness the Lord was drawing me.

It was 70's night and the youth group were dressed up and a disco ball hung from the ceiling. The worship leader had fake chest hair coming from his polyester shirt and people greeted me with smiles and it immediately felt good. It was like I had stepped out from the shade and into the sunlight. I settled in my predetermined spot in the back row as the music began. As the familiar songs began to be sung, I recognized the guy playing the drums as an old friend from summer camp and it felt as if that was a confirmation that I was in the right place.

As the message began, it was as if the pastor was talking directly to me. The idea of God's unending grace taking hold in my mind in a completely new way. As he gave the altar call for those who needed to accept the grace of God the conviction of the Holy Spirit began to sweep over me and the warmth of God's presence soaked into my very soul and I rushed from my seat into the altar and fell on my face and wept. Two ladies who didn't know me from Adam spent nearly two hours on the floor praying for me and hugging me as the Lord took me through nearly a year of devastating pain. They didn't have to know the details to know my story. I was desperately in need of grace.

The Holy Spirit caused me to AWAKEN. The Holy Spirit brought to my remembrance many times over the past year that He was close when I didn't think He was. When He was watching out for me and I didn't even realize it. When He was stubbornly present even after I thought I had kicked Him out. It was as if that night, God took me on a journey through the last year from His perspective and I saw the entire situation through the eyes of a father who was desperately trying to care for His daughter who rejected Him at every turn. I broke under the realization that I had brought the majority of my pain on myself. I had chosen to see the death of my idea for what my life was going to look like as punishment from God or lack of care instead of trying to see the circumstances as those I could overcome or even come back from. I blamed Him for so much and I never even gave Him a chance to redeem any part of the story.

The truth is, my life never even really started until I learned what it was to die. Up until that point my faith was shallow and was determined and based on everything going the way I wanted and earning what I deserved. None of that is how God works. On the altar that night, I died to my rights. I died to my plans and my works.

I learned what it was to see life through the lens of someone who loves unconditionally and forgives without reservation. I learned that the power and presence of the Holy Spirit is key to understanding the heart of the Father. The Holy Spirit is not an inconsequential aspect of God, but rather an intentional, integral core element of the very fabric of the Lord's being. One that was specifically sent to demonstrate the myriad of qualities of the one true God to us directly. If I was going to RAISE UP, I was going to have to unlock the understanding and the power of the Holy Spirit in my own life.

We do ourselves a huge disservice by discounting the role of the Holy Spirit in our lives. It was the Holy Spirit who triggered my remembrance of true joy to draw me back into the arms of the Father and it is the Holy Spirit who is moving in each of our lives as we work to CULTIVATE a relationship with him. The term 'trinity' was coined by Theophiles of Antioch (Paul's home church) in the late 2nd century to describe the oneness of God in 3 distinct parts and affirm the Holy Spirit as evident from the beginning. In Genesis 1:1-2 we see God the father and God the Holy Spirit present in the same moment fulfilling 2 different roles. In John 1:1 we recognize the presence of Jesus at that same moment as well and this realization helps us quantify the nature of God present in 3 forms. He is able to do this because of the 3 primary "Omni's" of the Lord. He is omnipotent, omniscient and omnipresent. As I began to put the broken pieces of my life back together I recognized my need for these aspects of the Lord in my understanding and in practice.

RAISE UP

Omnipotent, meaning all powerful, is God's ability to act in strength and fullness in every aspect of our world. It is almighty, infinite in power and unlimited authority. In Luke 5:17-26, Jesus demonstrates his authority over both sin and the physical body in one single instance as a group of friends lowers a crippled man on a mat into a room filled with onlookers. Jesus forgives the sins in his spirit and heals his physical body right there by the supernatural power of the Holy Spirit. In Exodus 7, God demonstrates his power and authority over the earth and everything within it with the demonstration of the 10 plagues of Egypt. In Ephesians 6, the Holy Spirit's power is demonstrated in his authority over the supernatural attacks of the enemy and our internal mind, heart and thoughts as the armor of God. His all-powerful nature is demonstrated on our physical earth through the Holy Spirit's physical presence.

Omniscient, meaning all-knowing, is God's ability to see and know all truth in every aspect of our personal lives as well as every aspect of our eternal universe, both time and space. God has complete and unlimited knowledge, awareness and understanding; perceiving all things and being all wisdom in all circumstances. Psalm 139:1-18 (NIV) demonstrates the Trinity's ability to know us beyond human ability in the most beautiful way:

"You have searched me, Lord, and you know me. You know when I sit and when I rise; you perceive my thoughts from afar. You discern my going out and my lying down; you are familiar with all my ways. Before a word is on my tongue you, Lord, know it completely. You hem me in behind and before, and you lay your hand upon me. Such knowledge is too wonderful for me, too lofty for me to attain. Where can I go from your Spirit? Where can I flee from your presence? If I go up to the heavens, you are there; if I make my bed in the depths, you are there. If I rise on the wings of the dawn, if I settle on the far side of the sea, even there your hand will guide me, your right hand will hold me fast. If I say, "Surely the darkness will hide me and the light become night around me," even the darkness will not be dark to you; the night will shine like the day, for darkness is as light to you. For you created my inmost being; you knit me together in my mother's womb. I praise you because I am fearfully and wonderfully made; your works are wonderful, I know that full well. My frame was not hidden from you when I was made in the secret place, when I

was woven together in the depths of the earth. Your eyes saw my unformed body; all the days ordained for me were written in your book before one of them came to be. How precious to me are your thoughts, God! How vast is the sum of them! Were I to count them, they would outnumber the grains of sand - when I awake, I am still with you."

Omnipresent, meaning everywhere present or present everywhere at the same time demonstrates God's Holy Spirit ability to be universally aware and involved in every moment of time in every place simultaneously. My favorite verse that shows this is Jeremiah 23:24 - *"Who can hide in secret places so that I cannot see them?" declares the Lord. "Do not I fill heaven and earth?" declares the Lord."* (NIV)

The trouble with my younger faith was that it had yet to struggle with the questions of who God really was if He wasn't Santa Claus in the sky. My failure of faith PROVOKED me and I didn't like who I saw without the Lord leading my life. The journey of brokenness I walked, desperately needed the divine intervention of a God who was all powerful, all knowing and always present. My rediscovery of Him affirmed my faith that even in my most lonely, I was never alone. I know I am not the only one to need assurance that His Holy Spirit is with us always.

So, as He is God, the Holy Spirit is all powerful, all knowing and everywhere present. We can look at is as He is everywhere both known and unknown, invisible and manifest. The unknown, or invisible, Holy Spirit presence of God is known by faith because scripture says He is present. Even if we don't feel Him, we know by faith the Holy Spirit is present as exampled by many times in scripture.

Psalm 19:1-6 (ESV), *"The heavens declare the glory of God, and the sky above proclaims his handiwork. Day to day pours out speech, and night to night reveals knowledge. There is no speech, nor are there words, whose voice is not heard. Their voice goes out through all the earth, and their words to the end of the world. In them he has set a tent for the sun, which comes out like a bridegroom leaving his chamber, and, like a strong man, runs its course with joy. Its rising is from the end of the heavens, and its circuit to the end of them, and there is nothing hidden from its heat."*

RAISE UP

Romans 1:19-20 (ESV), "For what can be known about God is plain to them, because God has shown it to them. For his invisible attributes, namely, his eternal power and divine nature, have been clearly perceived, ever since the creation of the world, in the things that have been made, so that they are without excuse."

Acts 17:26-27 (ESV), "And he made from one man every nation of mankind to live on all the face of the earth, having determined allotted periods and the boundaries of their dwelling place, that they should seek God, and perhaps feel their way toward him and find him. Yet he is actually not far from each one of us."

Matthew 18:20 (ESV), "For where two or three are gathered in my name, there am I among them."

Isaiah 43:2-3a (ESV), "When you pass through the waters, I will be with you; and through the rivers, they shall not overwhelm you; when you walk through fire you shall not be burned, and the flame shall not consume you. For I am the Lord your God."

Isaiah 57:15b (ESV), "I dwell in the high and holy place, and also with him who is of a contrite and lowly spirit."

The known, or manifest, presence of the Holy Spirit is clearly demonstrated when you see and feel Him moving in a supernatural way because He has made Himself available to our senses in a tangible way. 1/3 of all modern-day Christians world-wide are spirit-filled, experiencers of the gifts of the spirit that empower our lives.

The Holy Spirit's manifest presence is evident in the conviction of sins, divine healing, miracles, prophecy, joy and so much more. These may be gifts you are familiar or unfamiliar with, but they have been markers of the presence of the one true God since the spirit descended on Jesus and remained on Him in John 1:32 (ESV), *"And John bore witness: "I saw the Spirit descend from heaven like a dove, and it remained on him."* This is the first time we see the Holy Spirit in a tangible way.

In Luke 3:16 (ESV), John the Baptist shares the word of the Lord - *"...I baptize you with water, but he who is mightier than I is coming, the strap of whose sandals I am not worthy to untie. He will baptize you with the Holy Spirit and fire."* This is the first indicator of the powerful emphasis the Holy Spirit has in Jesus' life. These statements drew me into a deeper relationship with the Lord as I wrestled with allowing the Holy Spirit of God to remain on me as He did with Jesus. It was the leap of faith required of me as I laid on that altar carpet and the Lord pieced me back together.

At the end of the first chapter of John, Jesus calls Nathaniel to be a disciple by demonstrating His power through a word of knowledge, and Nathaniel is shocked. In this moment, Jesus just casually tells Nathaniel that he will do even greater things than this. This statement has always blown my mind and, in attempting to reconcile my human weakness with Jesus' supernatural abilities, I realized my feeble nature outside of a supernatural God. My struggle with ADVANCING in the power of the Lord came from trying to do it in my own strength. The only way I could demonstrate the power of Jesus was with the empowering of the Holy Spirit.

In Ezekiel 37, we find ourselves following the prophet of God in a vision that would bring hope and clarity to the Israelite people who once again found themselves captive and broken. Now we wouldn't know anything about that would we? This valley of dry bones, as it's so well known, holds precious meaning to us even today. "Dry bones" can mean many things to each of us. Maybe it's a situation where you don't see a way out and everything is completely collapsed. Maybe there are no apparent answers to your dilemma, and you live life in crisis mode. Maybe all you have left is dashed dreams and hopes, barrenness & desolation. I lost a year of my life to these feelings. We aren't physically dead, but we nearly feel like it and much of it was even from our own choices. But God….

As God led Ezekiel in a vision, he saw a valley littered with very dry bones. He called him to speak to the brokenness and watch it be made new. He spoke life in the face of death and watched as God brought order from the chaos. And yet we're still missing something. Soldiers stood in formation filling the valley and yet they did not live. Lastly, God had Ezekiel call the breath of God, the spirit of the living God, into their lungs and they came fully alive.

RAISE UP

Most of us know what dry bones are in our lives and the Lord is calling us to raise up and speak to the dead things, new life. Many of us have things looking really beautiful and in order and yet the spirit of God is missing and it feels hollow & empty; without power. I didn't put my life back together, the Holy Spirit of God met me at that altar and showed me His omnipotent, omniscient, omnipresent reality and my life was forever changed by the breath of God.

Only the breath of God can cause our dry bones to RAISE UP! Only the breath of God can cause us to AWAKEN from our spiritual sleep. Only the breath of God gives us a deep desire to CULTIVATE a new relationship with the Lord. Only the breath of God PROVOKES a holy fear of the Lord in us that takes us from weak to strong. Only the breath of God calls us from standing at the ready, to ready to ADVANCE.

I understand brokenness and yet today, I understand wholeness as well. I got up from that altar and off of the roller coaster. I was truly changed and began to serve the Lord with my whole heart from the perspective of love and not of obligation or earning. I experienced the power of the Holy Spirit in a way that was undeniable and life altering. If you are not sure you have experienced this power for yourself, then I challenge you to seek out the manifest presence of the Lord. Seek the closeness of the almighty and experience his goodness for yourself.

As a new creation I was unsure how to move forward so I did all I knew to, I began to serve. I joined the church, and served faithfully and rediscovered my purpose in the Lord. In my faithfulness, it just so happened that the guy playing the drums that I recognized from church camp asked me out and almost 20 years of marriage, and 4 children later, we're serving the Lord in ways I never expected. God blew my mind with His faithfulness. God restored everything I ever lost and gave me so much more than I ever deserved in my husband and children. It hasn't been easy, but it has been worth it.

God has such beautiful stories written on our hearts and if we never allow His Holy Spirit the opportunity to illustrate them, we miss out on the fullness of our purpose. I pray today you allow the Holy Spirit new room in your heart and mind to speak truth, change perceptions and breathe new life into your very bones. I pray you experience His unlimited power and His precious presence every day of your lives. I pray for you to walk faithfully and for you to fearlessly Raise UP!

CHRISTY CATLIN

Reflect and Write Your Story
From Grief To Renewal

Reflect:

In what way does the personal story you've just read connect with your own experiences? Is there common ground between you and the author? Explore the emotions you felt while reading. Where do those feelings stem from and how are they connected to your personal story?

RAISE UP

Writing Prompt:

Explore the individuals who left a mark on your personal narrative; good or bad. Delve into those who orchestrated change, examining the qualities that defined their character. How did their unique attributes and actions shape the course of your story?

CHRISTY CATLIN

Scripture Connection:

Looking back, can you see where God was in this part of your story? Do any scriptures come to mind?

Chapter Three
Kelly Levatino

KELLY LEVATINO

Kelly's Struggle:
Confronting The Reality Of Depression

Hello.

My name is Kelly, and since I was 12 years old (which was 28+ years ago if you must know), I've shared my head space with an unwanted "house guest" called Depression.

I don't know what caused it initially. Maybe abnormal hormonal shifts during puberty. Maybe my brain adapted to being sad for an extended amount of time during middle school life. Maybe I'm genetically predisposed to experiencing depression. Maybe I wasn't fed enough Oreos as a child.

Whatever the cause, the result was that my brain almost entirely stopped making its own dopamine (one of our "happy hormones" for us non-scientists). Unfortunately, it would be decades before I discovered this fact.

I became a Christian when I was 16. It's vitally important for you to know that I was depressed before I became a Christian, and I was depressed after becoming a Christian. And no amount of spiritual maturing on my part changed the fact that I continued to wrestle Depression for control of my "home." It took me 7 years and a few good, persuasive friends to finally agree to talk to a counselor about things at age 19. That counselor helped convince me to go see my family physician who could prescribe medication if he thought it was necessary.

I was officially diagnosed with dysthymia, a long-term, high-functioning form of depression. It basically means you are depressed for years but can still get out of bed and "do life." Every once in a while, you might have an episode of major depression, which is the version of the illness that makes your body feel encased in a lead suit. Your bones hurt and just thinking about moving or doing anything exhausts you. Major

RAISE UP

depression is not the norm for those who suffer from dysthymia, but I have had the displeasure of experiencing it a couple of times.

In Sleepless in Seattle, a depressed Tom Hanks delivers a line that always comes to mind when I'm feeling the weight of depression. The radio host asks him what he's going to do to cope with the loss of his wife, and he replies, "Well, I'm gonna get out of bed every morning, breathe in and out all day long, then, after a while, I won't have to remind myself to get out of bed every morning and breathe in and out…" I love this line because it so succinctly captures what it feels like to live in depression. Many days I'd have to psych myself up to do the mundane…to push through the feelings…to breathe in and out…to put one foot in front of the other…and to believe and hope that one day, maybe, I wouldn't have to remind myself to do all the little things that come so effortlessly to those who aren't depressed.

There is no cure for depression, but talk therapy and antidepressant medications can help some people. So that's what I did. For the next 12 years, I tried many different kinds of antidepressants. I saw a multitude of counselors and physicians. But my "house guest" came and went without rhyme or reason. When he went, Depression never went far… At most he stepped out on the porch of my mind for a cigarette break, and, then, he got right back at it, disheveling the rooms of my brain.

I got married, graduated college, and had 2 babies, never succeeding at truly getting the upper hand on my illness. I did things, I just didn't have much joy. I was literally unable to feel positive emotions most of the time.

Some moments were better than others, especially those that involved my precious, snuggly, funny, cutie daughters. (Hi, Best Daughters in the World!) But consistent, sustained happiness and contentment eluded me. (And, just for fun, during my first pregnancy, Depression started inviting his twin friends, Anxiety and Panic Attack, over to play at my house sometimes. They still visit on occasion.)

As years went by, I often found solace in David's psalms. He really seemed to get what I was experiencing. Psalm 13 is a good example. (Allow me to mash the NIV, ESV, and Amplified versions together to propose the most impactful reading possible.)

"How long will You forget me, O Lord? Forever? How long will You hide Your face from me? How long must I wrestle with my thoughts and have sorrow in my heart day after day? How long will my enemy triumph over me? Consider and answer me, O Lord my God; lighten the eyes [of my faith to behold Your face in the pitch like darkness], lest I sleep the sleep of death, and my enemy will say, "I have overcome him," and my foes will rejoice when I fall." (Psalm 13:1-4)

Cheery so far, no?

It's important to point out David is speaking like this to God. I know that seems pretty self-explanatory, but it's worth mentioning because I have a hunch a lot of religious people and/or new believers don't understand we have the freedom to be transparent with the Lord.

David is depressed, and it seems he can't keep his overwhelming thoughts to himself anymore. Although maybe he has tried to keep his thoughts sorted out, and his emotions in check, verse 2 tells us he hasn't been successful. He's spinning his spiritual wheels, and he simply can't take it anymore.

I can relate to David's question, "How long must I wrestle with my thoughts?" When depression engulfs me, the first thing I do is try to figure out what has caused the depression to return this time. I spend days racking my brain, analyzing stressors, foolishly believing that if I can discover the cause, I'll be able to control the depressive feelings. But chemical depression can't be controlled by wrangling wayward thoughts. To extend the wrestling metaphor, there is no "pinning" depression. The wrestling match turns into a wrestling marathon that causes me to exclaim, like David, "How long, O Lord?!"

Now, David is not blaming God for whatever challenging circumstances he has found himself in that are causing his depression. And David is not being disrespectful toward God by expressing his feelings, albeit passionately. Yes, we're allowed and encouraged to be candid with the Lord, but we still must be mindful that He is God and we are not, and, therefore, He is due respect at all times.

David communicates his painful feelings of sorrow, neglect, and frustration, and then he asks the Lord to "lighten the eyes" of his faith to behold God's face in the utter darkness of his depression. That's an

RAISE UP

interestingly worded request. David understands his feelings are not necessarily reflective of reality. In other words, he knows he isn't seeing things the same way God sees them. He needs his vision adjusted. David feels forgotten and abandoned by God, but he knows he isn't. Why else would he continue to pray? If he truly believed God had left him, David wouldn't be calling out to Him anymore. As inaccurate as they may be, his feelings are still a powerful force that needs to be dealt with. So David asks God to refocus his heart. David asks for his faith to be refreshed and his spiritual eyes to be put back on God.

Why does David make this request of God? Perhaps because David knows he can't accomplish this feat himself. In the throes of depression, David doesn't have the strength nor the willpower to "pull himself up by his bootstraps" and "turn that frown upside down". Being clinically depressed is not the same time as having a bad day or being bummed out. Depression is a debilitating disease.

David asks the Lord to "lighten his eyes" because he can't possibly lighten them himself. If you've ever been around a depressed person, you know this is true. There is no light in their eyes – no hope or faith that things will turn around for them – and no amount of them wishing they had hope and faith can make it so. When old pictures pop up in my Facebook "memories" each day, I can tell immediately by looking at my eyes if I was depressed when a photo was taken. There was always a smile on my face, but, when I was depressed, my eyes were tired and dim. Shakira says hips don't lie. Well, I say eyes don't lie.

David knows if God doesn't correct his eyesight–i.e., restore hope to his soul by refocusing his vision on the Lord–he WILL be overcome. David is in a desperate place, and, in a very literal way, his life is at stake. I don't know that we can go so far as to say David's lament that he will "sleep the sleep of death" if God doesn't rescue him from his depression is an indication that he may have been suicidal. But I don't know that we can rule that out, either. Most of the commentaries like to think of this as a reference to spiritual death–David's soul will be so utterly overwhelmed if the Lord doesn't deliver him that he will be as good as dead. In either case, David's life will be profoundly changed for the worse, either literally, through physical death, or spiritually, through spiritual collapse.

I still remember feeling this same level of hopelessness years ago, lying on my back on the floor, talking to the Lord as tears ran down the sides of my face and dripped into my hair. I remember closing my eyes and resting my interlocked hands on my forehead and just letting it all happen. Tears and prayer and labored breaths. A thousand thoughts and questions for God. I wasn't angry, but my tears wanted to know, why is this illness allowed to keep coming back, attacking my mind and my body, putting me through suffering and torment not unlike the physical suffering and torment patients experience when they have recurring cancer diagnoses?

We may never know the specific reasons why God allows certain painful things to happen in our lives, but we can always know a general reason: God allows pain because it drives us to move closer to Him. It's an unfortunate fact, but, when things go well for humans, we tend to neglect our relationship with God. We forget how much we need Him. But when we are hurting, we tend to turn to Him in prayer, worship, and scripture reading.

[Note: on its face, this sounds selfish of God. He lets us suffer because He wants to spend time with us?! RUDE. Of course, nothing with God is ever that simple. Yes, He wants to spend time with us. But that's not the only reason He wants us to come to Him. Being that He is super smart, He knows the best place for us–for our good–is with Him. It benefits us most when we are living in an active relationship with Him. And God is all about doing what is best for us. If that means He has to allow us to suffer to get us to come to Him, then that is what He will do. And when I think about my suffering depression in those terms, I am reminded God truly does love me, not in spite of His allowing my depression, but because He allows it.]

I imagine David asked the same question in his situation: "Why, God?" But, just when this psalm couldn't get any graver, David pens this conclusion: *But I have trusted, leaned on, and been confident in Your mercy and loving-kindness; my heart shall rejoice and be in high spirits in Your salvation. I will sing the Lord's praise, for he has been good to me.* (Psalm 13:5-6; an interpretation of NIV, ESV, and Amplified versions)

RAISE UP

Wait, what? Where did that come from?

In verse 4 David is on the brink of spiritual annihilation, and in verse 5 he is skipping through fields of wildflowers with Pharrell's "Happy" as his soundtrack. This is about the point I want to shut my Bible and say, "I can't even." David and I had been tracking together just fine until now…Right after he says he can't pull himself up by his bootstraps, he does?!

No, I don't think this change of heart came from David's can-do attitude. Remember, he just got done communicating he doesn't have what it takes to overcome his thoughts and sorrow himself. He needs God in the worst way! David's sudden change of heart wasn't of his own doing. Rather, I think it was a direct answer to David's prayer in verses 3-4 for God to "consider him." (I legitimately wonder how much time passed between David recording his plea with the Lord to deliver him from his depression in verse 4 and his inspirational self-pep-talk in verses 5 and 6. I'm thinking DAYS. It reads like it happened instantaneously, but I suspect it didn't.)

The Lord answered David's request to refocus his heart on God by empowering David to recall God's trustworthiness, dependability, mercy, and unfailing loving-kindness, as well as by reminding David of his salvation and other blessings from the Lord. No matter how long it did or did not take for David's tune to change, the Lord raised him up out of his depression by directing him to meditate on these things.

You and I can take a page out of David's book when we're flat on our backs emotionally. We can be honest with the Lord–passionately and transparently, yet respectfully honest–about how we're feeling when we're down. And we can fervently ask the Lord to "lighten our eyes" and refocus our hearts on Him. And then–and this is my favorite part–we can wait for the Lord to lift us from our sadness by empowering us like He did David to think truthful, helpful thoughts.

We don't have to get ourselves together! Isn't that the best news?!

Frankly, most of the time we can't get ourselves together, especially when it comes to being clinically depressed. But God can. He did it for David time and time again (see Psalms 42, 43, and 55 for more examples), and He can do it for us, too!

God can use a myriad of tools to raise us up out of depression. He may decide to instantly heal us if we ask Him to, or, as in my experience, He may use professionals, medications, therapies, family, friends, His Word, and the Holy Spirit over a looooooong period of time to raise us up.

God used my favorite therapist in all the world (and now my good friend!) to raise me up from the pit. (Hey, Linda!) Talking to a therapist actually takes more strength and humility (both good Christian virtues) than staying home all day in your pajamas, sullenly wishing Taco Bell delivered. But working with a professional who understands the truth about our souls as well as our brains can help you unravel and survive depression as a Christian.

God also used a psychiatrist to show me doctors who did not specialize in psychiatry had been targeting the wrong chemical in my brain at too low of a dose for years, hence my never making a whole lot of emotional progress while on various medications. When my brain finally got what it needed medicinally, my world changed in just 48 hours. It literally only took 2 days of being on the correct medicine for Depression to be evicted from my house! Finding the right medication, if your type of depression warrants it, can take a year or more, but if you're willing to work faithfully with a psychiatrist, God can use medication to raise you up.

Maintaining relationships is difficult and exhausting when you're depressed. But surrounding yourself with a handful of people that are willing and able to remind you they love you just as much when you are at your lowest as they do when you are at your best is essential. God used countless people over the years who acknowledged my feelings of hopelessness and my belief that there would be no end to the darkness while simultaneously reminding me, ever so gently, that light would come again. (Hey, Countless People!)

Over the last 19+ years of my relationship with depression, God has particularly used my amazing husband to help deliver me from the worst of it. (Hi, Amazing Husband!) Having a depressed spouse means more than just having to pull more than your fair share of household chores and parental responsibilities, although it does mean that. It also

RAISE UP

means having to watch the person you love most in the world suffer and not being able to help them. It means not understanding what they are going through (if you don't also have a history of depression), and it means feeling isolated in your own home. It means having to walk a thin line between protecting your spouse's privacy and satisfying inquiries from friends about why your wife isn't at social events with you. And it means having to get counsel yourself about how to best help your spouse and how to tend to your own negative feelings that your spouse's depression has caused you. Depression is brutal on marriages. I thank God for His grace to me and my husband during our struggle with my mental health.

    Maintaining your relationship with God is also difficult for the depressed. But telling Him exactly what you're feeling and thinking and continuing to read the Bible keeps the line of communication open. God used the depressing Psalms (like 13, 42, 43, and 55, for starters) to show me people in the Bible felt depressed, too, and most of the depressing Psalms end with the depressed person praising God! It is possible to praise when we are depressed.

    Another way God raised me up was by teaching me to give myself permission to rest. Depression is exhausting. Our bodies and brains need extra rest to recover from daily life. Note: I am NOT saying retreat. If you drop out of all your usual activities and hole up in your house, you're not "resting", you're "retreating", and you're going to sink deeper into depression than you ever have before because that's what happens when you're alone all the time. By forcing myself to attend something (like a Bible study or a church service or a family get-together) once a week and talk to someone while I was there, I stayed in touch with people, which is a balm to the depressed soul. And then I'd go home and eat Oreos and take a nap because I needed it, and I had done well that day.

    All of these things can help. And when they do, we praise God for His faithfulness in helping us through dark times via these means. We do not praise these things for helping us through. We worship the Creator, not the created. God may use people, doctors, medications, therapies, Bible studies, naps, and Oreos to alleviate some of our emotional distress, but those things in and of themselves are not God and would not work without His enabling them to do so.

KELLY LEVATINO

I am blessed to report that 7+ years ago God raised me up out of depression! I am fully aware Depression could come for a visit in the future, but, as of now, it seems I have been delivered long term. "I sought the Lord, and he answered me and delivered me from all my fears," (Psalm 34:4, NIV). But when I sought the Lord, He didn't just zap depression away like a magic trick.

It turns out depression can cause people to develop unhealthy coping mechanisms. Getting on effective medication allowed me to have the energy and clarity to confront my mechanisms of choice. God led me down a long, difficult road of painful "pruning." I was hesitant to give up my unhealthy ways of dealing with negative feelings. But, like a good father, He kindly ripped them out of my life, "encouraging" me to call a spade a spade and to do the hard work of learning how to get through this stressful thing called life in healthy ways. And on the other side of doing that work, by His grace, Depression moved out of my house and very rarely comes back to visit.

As for the anxiety and panic attacks I touched on above, every once in a while my body still gets confused into thinking I am in physical danger when I am not. When that happens, my body goes into a fight or flight response that God gave me to protect me in times of legitimate danger–like when I run out of Oreos–at random times. My heart rate increases, my body temperature skyrockets, I feel claustrophobic and unable to breathe, and, worst of all, my mind tells me I will never feel normal again. I am stuck in this state with no power to control what my body is doing, or so my mind tells me. It can be quite scary if I don't focus on telling myself the truth: I am safe.

The nice thing (if there is one) about anxiety is that the Bible speaks to it in more than one place. To be honest with you, before I experienced panic attacks, I always read verses about anxiety from the standpoint of mild worry. But when the Lord put me in a season of frequent, debilitating panic attacks, I looked afresh at the "anxiety verses". Peter wrote a famous few lines on the subject:

"Humble yourselves, therefore, under God's mighty hand, that he may lift you up in due time. Cast all your anxiety on him because he cares for you. Be alert and of sober mind. Your enemy the devil prowls around like a roaring lion looking for someone to devour.

RAISE UP

Resist him, standing firm in the faith, because you know that the family of believers throughout the world is undergoing the same kind of sufferings. And the God of all grace, who called you to his eternal glory in Christ, after you have suffered a little while, will himself restore you and make you strong, firm and steadfast. To him be the power for ever and ever. Amen." (1 Peter 5:6-11 NIV)

      Peter wrote this letter to believers who were experiencing persecution for following Christ. While my reason for having anxiety is not because I am being persecuted for my faith, the instructions Peter gives are still helpful.

Verse 6: "Humble yourselves, therefore, under God's mighty hand, that he may lift you up in due time."

We are to submit to the idea that our anxiety (however we experience it: mild worry, obsessive worry, depression, panic attacks, debilitating anxiety disorders, etc.) is God's doing (either directly or indirectly); He is in control. He is sovereign over the situation. God knows what's best, and, as hard as it is, He has deemed experiencing anxiety best for us when we are having it. And He is trustworthy; He will deliver us from this suffering at the proper time.

Verse 7: "Cast all your anxiety on him because he cares for you."

We are to continually place our anxiety on Him, not keep it ourselves. Whether it's worrisome thoughts or physical anxiety, we should consciously give those things to God. We can do this through simple prayer: "Lord, I don't want to worry about ____. I don't want to be afraid of ____. I don't want to feel ____. You take these things."

      I have a hunch that if God tells us to cast our anxiety on Him, it's because He is willing to take it from us. In other words, it will be a fruitful exercise. He cares for us! As alone as we may feel amid anxiety, the truth is we are not alone. And because He cares about us, He wants our anxiety. He wants to free us from all levels of worry, just as we long to ease our children's worried minds and take their physical pain from them.

Verse 8: "Be alert and of sober mind. Your enemy the devil prowls around like a roaring lion looking for someone to devour."

Satan wants to devour us in the midst of our experiencing anxiety. This is an opportune time for him. I don't know that he can cause our anxious symptoms (particularly physiological responses), but I am certain he tries to exacerbate them by drumming up our fears.

Satan is called the father of lies in John 8:44. He lies to us, hoping we will get anxious and stay anxious. Two lies he loves to bait me with when I am experiencing physical symptoms of anxiety is that I am in danger and there will be no end to these symptoms. He tries to convince me I need help, but no one can help. He wants me to believe the torture will last forever.

In instances of anxiety, we need to say to Satan, "I will not be the one you devour!" We literally need to say those words out loud because, unfortunately, Satan is real, demons are real, and they are looking to devour you and me.

Verse 9a: "Resist him, standing firm in the faith…"

We can resist Satan by declaring the truth out loud, "God is good. He only allows that which is in my best interest. I refuse to believe otherwise. He is in total control, and I am safe with Him." (Psalm 107:1, Romans 8:28, Proverbs 19:21, Psalm 4:8) Verbally recalling God's good character traits and reading aloud Bible verses that speak to reality reorients us to the truth.

Verse 9b: "…because you know that the family of believers throughout the world is undergoing the same kind of sufferings."

We are not alone! Believers all over the world and all over our own churches are experiencing the same kinds of suffering, including anxiety.

As a side note, Satan seeks to divide and conquer by isolating us (remember how I said we can rest, but we can't retreat?). The more we

RAISE UP

share our stories with one another, the braver we all become in getting the help we need to overcome our anxiety, especially the more debilitating forms.

Verse 10: "And the God of all grace, who called you to his eternal glory in Christ, after you have suffered a little while, will himself restore you and make you strong, firm and steadfast."

Though we suffer, we can take heart that we will not suffer forever. We are personally called and chosen by God; God Himself will restore us from our seasons of suffering. (Does that remind you of David's plea for God Himself to "lighten" David's eyes? It should. If it doesn't, you missed the gist of the first half of this chapter. -100 points.) And when God restores us to emotional health, He will make us strong, firm, and steadfast. There are no mincing words here; this is a promise!

Verse 11: "To him be the power for ever and ever. Amen."

It is by God's power and as a testament to His power that these things will come to pass. Amen is an expression of absolute confidence that it will be so! Peter is confident. We can be confident.

Living with mental illness is far from easy. But there is hope. His name is Jesus, and He has the power to raise you up! If you find yourself in a dark place, consider the words of Paul:

"And we know that in all things God works for the good of those who love him, who have been called according to his purpose. For those God foreknew he also predestined to be conformed to the image of his Son, that he might be the firstborn among many brothers and sisters. And those he predestined, he also called; those he called, he also justified; those he justified, he also glorified. What, then, shall we say in response to these things? If God is for us, who can be against us? He who did not spare his own Son, but gave him up for us all—how will he not also, along with him, graciously give us all things?" (Romans 8:28-32 NIV) ~Amen.

KELLY LEVATINO

Reflect and Write Your Story
Confronting The Reality Of Depression

Reflect:

In what way does the personal story you've just read connect with your own experiences? Is there common ground between you and the author? Explore the emotions you felt while reading. Where do those feelings stem from and how are they connected to your personal story?

RAISE UP

Writing Prompt:

Did the choices of others dictate the course of your life or were they decisions of your own? Detail the ways these decisions molded the path you were on. What are some of the emotions and thoughts while navigating this situation?

KELLY LEVATINO

Scripture Connection:

Looking back, can you see where God was in this part of your story? Do any scriptures come to mind?

Chapter Four
Liz Catlin

Liz's Story:
Defeating Dysfunction

Isaiah 59:19 "So they shall fear the name of the Lord from the west, and his glory from the rising of the sun. When the enemy shall come in like a flood, the Spirit of the Lord shall lift up a standard against him." (KJV)

I was at my mother's funeral when the stark realization of the term "RAISING UP A STANDARD" hit me. Now let me quickly point out that funerals in our family look completely different than those of most. Funerals tend to be somber events with tears shed and memories shared. My family...not so much. We give a whole new meaning to the word dysfunctional, and it's never more evident than at family funerals. While some others may have experienced a form of hysterics at a funeral, we have comedic hysterics; to the point of some attendees having suggested we should sell tickets, much like those sold for comedy shows. I kid you not... and my mother's funeral was the most over the top parody of somber ever witnessed by most.

Cue the carnival music! The circle that was her funeral began with an encounter with someone identifying herself as my mother's best friend. She was dressed in cut off jeans and flip-flops. Her top was a makeshift cover for nothing but nakedness underneath, made from a men's sleeveless tee with the neckline cut out in order to provide a place to hang her keys. This grief-stricken woman, most likely years younger than her furrowed face portrayed, was genuinely upset over losing my mother and had sought me out to express her deepest sympathy.

In hindsight, I probably wasn't the most gracious. I was so taken aback by the people filling up the funeral home. It was such a paradox...the absurdity of which wasn't lost on other relatives who hadn't seen my mother in a long time, me included. Understand, our

RAISE UP

family has always been one to exercise proper and discrete behavior in public, even while carefully hiding the skeletons in the closets in private... so this spectacle of bizarre attendees, sincerely mourning her passing, had us all in somewhat of a daze. Apparently the last several years of her life were spent cultivating friendships, authentic friendships it would seem; in a world I have zero point of reference. A world that gives new meaning to the word transient...yet somehow these people earnestly feel as if they have some sort of lifelong connection to each other. Maybe because they are craving something real to fill the void in their lives and having no understanding of a relationship with God, they cling to whoever is closest at the moment? I just don't know.

As I sat mostly incredulous, taking in the sights and sounds....oh my, the sounds, as people filed in and milled about, I couldn't help but wonder how in the world I had come from this woman. The old Sesame Street song "One of These Things Doesn't Belong Here" sprang to my mind. And yet it was there, among a crowd of the strange, weird and odd, that God pulled back the curtain to show me an "It's a Wonderful Life" glimpse of what could have been and what should have been in my own life. But thankfully, because He miraculously intervened, my path went in a completely different direction than the lost people circulating among me.

Thirty-two years earlier, my timid and soft spoken mother had listed her husband as my father on my birth certificate... a detail that couldn't have been further from the truth. Anyone could see there was no way the six foot five inch, full-blooded Cherokee Indian and the petite, black-haired, bright blue-eyed woman in the casket had produced a green-eyed, red-headed baby girl, who suspiciously looked exactly like my mother's high school sweetheart!

There is a saying that "truth is relative", and depending on which of my relatives you asked about any given subject, is the truth you get! It wasn't until I was thirteen that I found out the truth of my parentage. As you can imagine, thirteen is a volatile age to discover something so disconcerting about your identity. Apparently I had always been skeptical though, that the man others referred to as my dad truly was. I say "others referred to" because from the time I could talk until it was confirmed to me that in fact he wasn't biologically my father, I never would call him "Dad". It just wouldn't form on my lips. Not because of anything he had done; it just didn't feel...true. Come to find out-it wasn't. While he had always known the truth and I was to find out eventually, neither of us ever mentioned it. He treated me no differently than his bio kids...probably better! Some of them are real characters.

He was an amazing man with a huge capacity to love unconditionally! As evidenced by the love and affection he showed me even while knowing I wasn't his child. Oh, and then there were his seven marriages to attest to his ability to distribute affection. Had he decided to go for eight, he would have had to leave the state of Texas to do so...apparently the powers that be, decided seven was the magic number here. Luckily, wife number seven was the one to keep him in matrimonial bliss. But that entire story is a book for another time. Suffice to say, growing up in all of that chaos would cause anyone to question their identity, right?

BUT GOD! In His infinite mercy and grace, He delivered me at a very young age, 13 months old to be exact, into the caring hands of my maternal grandmother and her husband. They painstakingly brought me up in a household one would consider completely normal; especially given the contrasting environment I was born into. My parents would both later go on to marry and divorce others, and find themselves in addictions and black holes hard to crawl out of. My siblings would suffer the consequences of parental choices as well, both having dealt with their own demons of substance abuse. I'm certain my role of overseer at my mother's funeral was suggestive of my sibling's inability to manage the situation. I barely knew our mom, much less the people she surrounded herself with, while my brothers had spent the greater part of their lives with her. I was completely out of my depth that day, but I did the best I could with what was thrown at me...and it was a lot.

As soon as the service began I knew we were in for a long day...the officiate leading the service mispronounced her name over and over. Seriously! How difficult is MARIE? Apparently it was for him; he just couldn't pull it off. This, coupled with my earlier encounter with her "best friend", and now sitting for what seemed an eternity among a large turnout of mourners, who collectively sounded as if they too were dying of what had killed her - years of smoking and drinking - it started me giggling. And not just a brief chuckle...it turned into the "hide your face in your hands, tears streaming, shoulder shaking, extreme case of giggles!

RAISE UP

It was at this point of the service where everyone files past the coffin and out the door, headed towards the processional line; but many who were witnessing what they thought was a grieving daughter, would stop to console me. This only resulted in more laughter and shaking and I couldn't possibly make eye contact or else I would give myself away! It was a vicious cycle! At one point our Pastor who had come to the service, leaned over and whispered into my ear almost verbatim what I had asked myself earlier- "How in the world did you come from this family?" God does have a sense of humor and it was never more evident than that day.

Webster's Dictionary defines "STANDARD" as - A general consent as a model or example. This is what we all incorporate into our daily lives, for the good, the bad, or the ugly. Every one of us has some sort of standard we use to measure our lives. The decisions we make, our choices, the friends we align ourselves with, the spouse we select and the ideologies we embrace...everything about us is based upon that standard. Read the definition again. "A general consent." Consent. It's what we give permission, approval, authority....to rule our lives. Scary huh?

As Christ-followers, we are called to walk according to the standard or model that Jesus has set for us according to the word of God and the leading of His Holy Spirit. My mother had chosen her own standard. In all of the time I knew her, she had never made the decision to invite Jesus into her life. I didn't know her to be a bad person though; remember I said she was timid and soft spoken? And her funeral was attended by caring and sorrowful people, who would genuinely miss her.

But in a world of ever changing values and moral ambiguities, more often than not, culture sways our perspectives easily if we aren't rooted in God's word. My mother and her friends may have been the nicest, most caring people ever, but without a relationship with Jesus it was all for nothing. Psalms 144:4 (ESV) tells us *"Man is like a breath; his days are like a passing shadow."*

Over the years, I have had time to process most of my thoughts about that day...In the beginning I was just amused. Amusement turned into all out wonderment, as other extended family members succumbed to illness and accidents. Sitting through each of their memorial services I was again struck with a sense of disbelief that people actually live and behave in such a way as to have no real awareness of God.

While my grandparents weren't believers until much, much, later in their lives, they were both very moral people, having been raised on "The Golden Rules". The Ten Commandments have always set concise and powerful guidelines to the older generations. Many though, while they believed in God, didn't necessarily believe in having a daily relationship with Him. He was just this huge presence in the heavens somewhere; someone you prayed to when you needed something you couldn't get on your own. Someone you threatened your children with, kind of like Santa Claus...or someone who made you feel uncomfortable when you skipped church. There are more "don'ts than do's" in this type of relationship. Again, my grandparents were wonderful people, benevolent and gracious, but spiritually lost like the rest of the family none the less. Thankfully, they were not trapped in the poverty mentality that my parents were.

It's this "poverty mentality" that catches my attention often since those days of attending the funerals of fruitless lives. With each one, I recognized the Spirit of Deficiency. I may not have known what to call it at the time, but as I grew in wisdom and discernment in the things of God, it became noticeably clear to me what the stronghold was in my family, and how destructive it had been for generations.

That's what a Strongman does; he works his way patiently and patently down through generations of families until he is met with resistance. Webster's definition of "strongman" is "one who leads or controls by force of will". When we haven't submitted our will to God, it goes to Satan by default. As far as I know, no one in my family had submitted their entire life to Jesus until I came along. There may have been those I am unaware of, in generations past, that had called out to the Lord with their last breath, (a prayer I have prayed many times over for my mother-"Please Lord let her have cried out for you in her last moment"...something I won't know until I too make that journey and see for myself if she's there) but the Strongman had exercised control over both sides of my immediate family for a long time.

The glaring difference between my mother's life and my own? It wasn't just the poor choices she had made in her fifty-four years of existence. I have made plenty of my own bad choices. Nor was it her

RAISE UP

decision to abandon her children and responsibilities in order to seek out fulfillment in sordid relationships. No, it was her inability to see herself as anything other than her own Savior. That sounds funny to say it that way, because looking at her life, one would think she would have had a pitiful opinion of herself and her circumstances, but no. In her deficiency she was unable to. This same deficiency that creates a poverty mentality isn't just for lack of resources...it's for lack in everything! This spirit steals your finances, your families and finally your faith; your very ability to trust God!

    This life certainly presents us with a host of various challenges that test our resilience and character. These trials are to point us to the cross of Jesus. The Bible is full of people who faced adversities, but with courage and unwavering faith; much like Job. Ironically, many of my mother's circumstances mirror his. The difference was Job never wavered from his faith whereas my mother never activated hers. I was so incredibly blessed, for reasons I can't comprehend, that God plucked me from the mire that could have been my life with my parents, placed me in a home where I was loved and nurtured...A home that, while not filled with the presence of God, had "parents" that wanted the best for me. In their desire to see me thrive, they unwittingly surrendered me to the Lord's will instead of theirs. I think this happened because of my opening verse - Isaiah 59:19 (KJV), *"So they shall fear the name of the Lord from the west, and His glory from the rising of the sun. When the enemy shall come in like a flood, the Spirit of the Lord shall lift up a standard against him."* Not that my grandparents so much "feared the name of the Lord" at that time in their lives, but it's in the last part of the verse..."*When the enemy shall come in like a flood, the Spirit of the Lord shall raise up a standard against him.*" (Isaiah 59:19b, KJV)

    For generations the enemy had come in like a flood, on both sides of my family. Substance abuse ran rampant, as did violent behavior resulting in many being incarcerated. I think every man on my dad's side going back for at least five generations, has seen the inside of prison walls at some point. I've already told you about the marital discord, all stemming from infidelity and unfaithfulness; unfaithfulness to spouses and to God. The female family line had also gone back at least five generations with affairs and abandoning not only their vows, but their families in some instances.

LIZ CATLIN

BUT GOD! In His infinite grace, mercy, and omniscience, He desired to raise the standard in my family and it started with me.

I describe my conversion story quite oddly; I guess that is fitting with the rest of my story, right? There is a country and western song called "Little Girl", by John Michael Montgomery. Apparently it's not a true story, but in some ways it describes very accurately my young life and my coming to know Jesus. The gist of the story in the song is this: a little neglected girl, born to a volatile couple, witnesses her parent's death and is relocated to a foster family. Her new parents are Christ followers and take her to church. The first Sunday, she is introduced to Jesus. It's at that point she realizes she recognizes Him as the Angel who kept her safe during all of the ugliness in her previous home.

At the age of six, I was introduced to Jesus at Vacation Bible School. I had started kindergarten at a private school that year, and while there was focus on God, it wasn't until VBS that summer that I met Jesus. I don't remember much about the "who and how" but I do remember the ladies there being very different than the school teachers and even the Pastor who presided over the chapel services. Where they all appeared so formal, these ladies acted as if they truly liked this guy Jesus. And the snow cones at the end of the day were a real treat! It was during this week of properly being introduced to Him that I realized I had known Him for a while...just didn't know WHO He was. I knew there was "someone" I talked with often; my grandparents even had commented on it. I also knew that when I felt Him I felt safe and not scared. (Even as I type that sentence I get weepy, knowing I still am the little girl who needs to feel safe and only feels that way in His presence). Now I had a name and His story.

Shortly after that, our neighbors, who loved the Lord and kind of evangelized the area we lived in, had asked my Grandma if they could take me to church. Surprisingly she said yes! Understand, this was a woman who was intensely over protective! She had experienced many losses in her life and she was extremely vigilant of me. For her to consent to this couple taking me anywhere from her presence was HUGE! I know beyond a shadow of a doubt this was miraculous in some way. It was at this little Baptist church I began to learn the Word of God. Memorizing scriptures out of my little zippered children's Bible became my favorite activity. I still have that Bible, along with many others - I have become a

RAISE UP

collector of God's word. As I grew in stature, both in height and character, it became almost second nature to me to be conscientious of not disappointing either God or my grandparents; I was kind of a model child and teen. I loved church and even though I was the only one in my home attending, I couldn't wait to get there! I loved the people because they seemed so different than those I was surrounded by. I realize now of course that many were on their best behavior at church and probably lived their everyday life very close to what I was used to away from church. But at the time, the term "Christian" held such an elevated position in my mind.

Although church and Jesus made a very early impression upon me, I haven't always done everything right. I too succumbed to the same generational curse that plagued the women in my family line. My standard may have been higher than some in my family, but at some point in my early adulthood I had stopped examining my flaws and my daily need for repentance; I began walking for a time in the same pride of life my own mother did, yet not recognizing it. That's what happens when you take your eyes off Jesus, if even for a short time. The enemy has a standard too! Remember he comes in "like a flood"! In just an instant, he can swoop in and swallow you up with a wave of tumultuous destruction-just ask Peter. When he took his eyes off Jesus, he began to sink into the ocean's depths. When we leave a door open for the devil to just get a foothold, he will yank that door off the hinges!

A few years after my self-sabotage, God was doing what He does best–making a way where there isn't any. My marriage was slowly being restored; trust is the most difficult thing to earn back. My children were, at the time, thankfully too young to realize what had happened, although, as adults I would later tell them everything in order to help them avoid the same snares the enemy would most undoubtedly try and set for them. I was sincerely repentant, praying constantly for those I had hurt with my selfishness and painfully disbelieving that I could have done something so blatantly stupid and cruel. And yes, I wondering if God would ever use me again for Kingdom purposes; I certainly didn't deserve His consideration. It was in the midst of this mental mire that I had the dream.

The scene was a hospital delivery room. It was very stark and sterile, as you can imagine, and smelled of disinfectant. My mother lay on the bed, in the throes of childbirth, surrounded by the appropriate hospital personnel. There was a very tall and very masculine man at her bedside; he was dressed in normal clothes but I knew that he was an angel. He just stood there taking it all in. I knew from that dream, and others that the Lord would speak to me through in the future, that God had a purpose for me way before I could have ever imagined. God tells us in His word, "*I knew you before I formed you in your mother's womb. Before you were born I set you apart....*" (Jeremiah 1:5a, NLT)

    Now understand, I tell this dream for one reason only...to help you understand how special you are! I am no more important or special than any one of you reading this. BUT GOD, in His infinite wisdom has created a time span for every person He puts in the mother's womb. You and I have been created and positioned truly "for such a time as this". What are we going to do with it? This supernatural purpose we have been born into? Because THAT is our true raise up story; all of us!!

    I don't understand why God rescued me when He did, for this truly is a rescue story. Probably because my life would have skewed way off course had He not stepped in when He did. But I know we have all been created to change the world in some capacity. Ephesians 2:10 (NIV) says, "*For we are God's handiwork, created in Christ Jesus to do good works, which God prepared in advance for us to do.*" He has raised us up. Don't let the enemy steal your raise up story by questioning God's methods; His ways are so much higher than ours. I have heard powerful testimonies, like those of Beth Moore and Joyce Myers, whose raise up stories look far different from my own, and were tragic. Yet God has used these women and their stories to give hope to millions of others around the globe.

    We have been positioned and seated to be a light that reflects His goodness. 1 Peter 2:9 (ESV) states, "*But you are a chosen race, a royal priesthood, a holy nation, a people for his own possession, that you may proclaim the excellencies of him who called you out of darkness into his marvelous light.*" He has awakened us to who we are in Christ. We have been charged by the Holy Spirit to live and love graciously, with the mercy of Christ. Psalm 139:23-24 (NIV), "*Search me, God, and know my heart; test me and know my anxious thoughts. See if there is any offensive way in me, and lead me in the way everlasting."* He wants us to cultivate relationships in His image.

Like Jesus, we are to frustrate the powers of darkness and to excite believers into action. This is one of my favorite things in life-A CALL TO PROVOKE! You may read that as negative but it's not. The definition of provoke is to stimulate a reaction. My prayer is that every believer reacts. Hebrews 10:24-25 (KJV),"*…and let us consider one another to provoke unto love and to good works: not forsaking the assembling of ourselves together, as the manner of some is; but exhorting one another: and so much the more, as ye see the day approaching."* We are to build up the faith in each other by provoking a faith reaction! And lastly, He has called us to advance His kingdom. Matthew 6:33 (NIV) tells us, "*But seek first his kingdom and his righteousness, and all these things will be given to you as well."*

Do you see the pattern in all of these? It's the pattern of raising a standard. I could have continued down the road of the low standard my mother had set for herself...that those before her had as well. And while my foot slipped into the snare for a brief time, I quickly regained my footing because I had history with God and I refused to lower my standard to that of the enemy, because I was fashioned for greatness, and so are you!

Every one of us has a standard of life; our character is measured by this. As Christ-followers we are called to walk according to this yardstick or model that Jesus has set for us according to the word of God and the leading of His Holy Spirit. I talk a lot about God's grace and mercies, because those attributes of His have been my life lines for many years, through many trials. Grace and mercy are His standards in relationships. When God raises a standard, He is proclaiming who He is and what He is capable of doing! He's announcing what He stands for and we better take notice because it is a level of excellence.

When we live our lives according to the standard of God we are saying we are united with our King and His army...our principles are His principles. The flag we fly is the colors of His kingdom. It requires boldness and faith in the face of opposition and it also requires a moral excellence that some would rather shun and criticize.

LIZ CATLIN

As you can imagine, with how my life choices contradict those of most in my family, I've not been the most popular throughout the years, nor did I get invited to reunions or holiday gatherings. Some of that had to do with my parentage...stepmothers used the excuse to keep me and my family from get-togethers, even though they had no real proof my dad wasn't really "my dad." But again God was so faithful!

While I didn't have men in my life whose blood ran through me, I had a close relationship with the one whose blood meant the most! The older I got, the more important my relationship with God the Father became. He became my source of all things father related. It was Him I looked to for guidance...I continued to have conversations with Him as a teen and an adult, just like when I was a child, and our conversations have grown to encompass the majority of my dialogue daily. He never refuses my calls! He is my "dad" in every sense of the word as I understand it. He cares for me and protects me; He even sends bodyguards to watch over me (Angels). It's like being the daughter of a mob boss! He provides for me, calls me His daughter...He puts me first. What I mean by that is He always has my best interest in mind. Isn't that what a good Dad does? Looking back I realize I didn't miss out on a single thing.

Not only did God step in and model what a good father is, He gave me two men who loved me like their own, even though I wasn't. My grandmother's husband never had children of his own, so I became his and my children became his grandchildren. I was born into such incredible wretched dysfunction, yet God never missed a beat with His abundant supply of grace.

I've heard grace and mercy often described this way-Grace is getting something good you didn't deserve and Mercy is NOT getting something bad that you did deserve. We all deserved a life sentence in Hell for our sin...especially when we intentionally go against God like I did when I followed the path into generational destruction. But God had others plans for me...He has other plans for you.

No matter what you came from, what you've done, God's grace is sufficient. Think about it this way...God is omniscient, meaning He knows everything, past, present and future. And while He will not interfere in our free will, He did have choice in whether or not to create us. Remember the verse Jeremiah 1:5 - "*I knew you before I formed you in your mother's*

RAISE UP

womb..." (Jeremiah 1:5a, NLT). That tells us that He already knew all the things we would mess up; all the things we would get right; all the ways we would disappoint Him and things that would bring Him joy...our victories and our failures. And if you are like me, the failures have outweighed the victories many times. YET!!! He decided to create the both of us anyway. What an incredible thought! It blows my mind to think that the God who formed the universe wanted me in it. He wanted you in it too; right now!

In the years since my mother, my dad, and my grandparents have all passed away, I have had to do a deep dive into who I really am; who do I identify as? Am I just an abandoned little baby girl whose parents couldn't/wouldn't set aside their addictions to care for me? Am I an orphan who was just lucky enough to be adopted by my grandparents? Or maybe I am an illegitimate child with no real claim to a father figure. No, none of these, if Jeremiah 1:5 is true, because the end of that verse says "*I have set you apart.*"

Ladies, don't listen to the voice of the enemy; he is a liar. We have been set apart. God raised up a standard and that standard is us. He has raised us up to awaken, cultivate, provoke, but most of all, to advance! What are you doing to advance the Kingdom of God in your family? I refuse to lower my standards...the spiritual lives of my children and grandchildren depend upon high Godly standards. Until my dying breath, I will hold up a Godly yardstick for them to see and know that this Granny will always take their heritage seriously.

Pray this over your families and commit to raising and keeping a Godly standard in your home:

Father God, help me to raise the standard in my home, starting with me. Give me wisdom and guide me into all things that are of you. Show me where I have missed it; highlight the areas that need to be removed in my life and in my home. Give me discernment with my family; tell me how to pray for them and reveal the areas where there may be lack, fear, or any door that may be opened to the enemy. Awaken their hearts to the things of You and create in our home a desire to know You more. In Jesus' name, Amen.

Reflect and Write Your Story
Defeating Dysfunction

Reflect:

In what way does the personal story you've just read connect with your own experiences? Is there common ground between you and the author? Explore the emotions you felt while reading. Where do those feelings stem from and how are they connected to your personal story?

RAISE UP

Writing Prompt:

Think about the relationship you have with the Lord. Describe the circumstances that led you to know Him and how that journey unfolded. What names do you know Jesus by and why?

LIZ CATLIN

Scripture Connection:
Did the Holy Spirit reveal scriptures to you that resonated with your spirit?

RAISE UP

Chapter Five
Bev McCann

BEV MCCANN

Bev's Valleys:
Navigating Loss, Lies & Witchcraft

    I am a Christian, wife, mother, grandmother, singer, songwriter, musician, minister, and a small business owner. God has blessed me to be able to do what I love; sing and minister His word. I have a story to tell about how the grace and mercy of God brought me through difficult times and how it is possible to live in victory through the thunderous storms of life. You may look at the destruction, pain and scars in your own life and wonder "how can I overcome? How can I have victory?" I assure you, God's grace and mercy are not only able to heal and deliver you from your past, but God will also restore what was taken, like He did for Job (Job 42:12-15).

    I pray my story will fill you with hope and encouragement. I pray you will see that God will never leave you or forsake you and that, He will carry you through the storms of life to the hilltops of victory.

    Life is not always a bed of beautiful roses. Often, it seems to be full of thorny bushes. But, if we learn to trust the Lord with all our heart and see things through His eternal view, we can dance around the thorns and enjoy the beauty God has given us. Think of the good things of God today and enjoy every minute He has given you with your loved ones, friends, and family.

Philippians 4:8 (KJV), "Finally, brethren, whatsoever things are true, whatsoever things are honest, whatsoever things are just, whatsoever things are pure, whatsoever things are lovely, whatsoever things are of good report; if there be any virtue, and if there be any praise, think on these things."

Psalms 18:1-3 (KJV), "I will love thee, O'Lord my strength. The Lord is my rock, my fortress, and my deliverer; my God, my strength, in

RAISE UP

who I will Trust: my buckler, and the horn of my salvation, and my high tower. I will call upon the Lord, who is worthy to be praised;"

Psalms 18:1-3 is one of the many portions of scripture that help get me through life. God has been my strength and my buckler; especially during the past few years. I have learned to rise up and follow the Lord and His guidance; to not sit still and let the Devil win. I have never been good at losing. People who know me well might say I'm a bit (or maybe 'very') competitive.

Life is not a game. It is for keeps, with serious consequences like Heaven or Hell. But it is not just about where we end up; it is also about how we live. I have and will continue to face hard times. I am also blessed beyond measure. After long talks with my Heavenly Father, I decided that with His help, I was going to live in victory and not let the Devil have a foothold in my life or my family. You too can know that same peace and victory from God.

There is nothing our God cannot do and nothing He won't do for his children (Luke 1:37, Psalm 84:11). This is why we must anchor deep in the Word of God and find our resting place in Him, so we are able to stand firm and fight.

Growing up, I had a wonderful mom and dad. We were raised in a godly home, taught godly values, and I had a deep understanding of the power of the Holy Spirit and God's saving grace. I wish I could say my upbringing protected me from the trials of life, but it did not.

1 Peter 5:8 (TLB), "Be careful—watch out for attacks from Satan, your great enemy. He prowls around like a hungry, roaring lion, looking for some victim to tear apart."

John 10:10 (KJV), "The thief cometh not, but for to steal, and to kill, and to destroy: I am come that they might have life, and that they might have it more abundantly."

Even though I had wonderful parents and a great childhood, that didn't mean I was immune to attacks from the Devil, or that life's twists and turns skipped over me. In fact, I believe that when you have an anointing and calling on your life, the Devil puts a target on your back. Satan targeted me and tried to destroy me, just like he did to Job. Satan was jealous of God's blessings on Job, so he targeted him directly. When you serve God, you are a threat to the Devil because God's light in you leads people to his saving grace. Satan wants to steal, kill, and destroy. But thanks be unto God who gives life more abundantly.

Growing up in church was one of the great blessings in my life; one that I am forever grateful for. When I look back on my upbringing and the teachings and worship I experienced, I realize how big a role that played in making me who I am today. There is nothing quite like being in a service where the Holy Spirit has freedom to move, and to see lives saved, changed, and taken to a deeper place with God. Nothing this world has to offer can compare to the power of the Holy Spirit.

I got married at the tender age of 17, between my junior and senior years in high school. I asked my mom several years later, why she let us get married. Her reply was, "Well Beverly, you were just stubborn enough to run off and get married anyways." I often wondered how she knew that came up in our conversations. I guess my mom and God had been talking.

My marriage was not the fairy tale I thought it would be. Don't get me wrong, we had good times. I loved him, and I believe he loved me too. But there were things we weren't prepared for; or maybe I wasn't prepared for. I was not prepared for arguments and flying remotes and dishes. (Thank God I was young and had good reflexes.) I had no idea people lived like that. I was either sheltered or blessed as a child; I believe I was blessed. My parents never fought. We might have heard "Now Mama?" or "Now Ray?" every once in a while, but I never heard my parents raise their voices at each other. They always showed each other respect and love.

I remember sometimes after a fight or disagreement, I'd be crying or upset, and my son would put his little arms around me and say, "It's okay mommy, I love you". Moments like that gave me courage to go on. God will do that for us every day if we allow Him to. He loves us so much that He sent His Son to die on a cross so we can have eternal life. Wow, that's some kind of love, isn't it? In the Sermon on the Mount, Jesus described how much the Heavenly Father cares for the "fowls of the air," to let us know how much more He will do for us (Matt. 6:26). I recorded a song called, "How Much More," written by Rusty Goodman. It is a

RAISE UP

beautiful song that I wish I could have written. It is about how much more God loves us than all His other creations. You are loved by God.

My first marriage lasted 13 years. I felt like I was living on a rollercoaster; a good week, or month or even year, then down we went. It was dizzying. I remember talking with my Pastors who, like my parents, were a wonderful blessing in my life. Sister H, would tell me, "Bev it will get better, just hold on." We would pray and I'd hold on. She told me to just wait, after 7 years it will get better, and it did for a while. Then the roller coaster ride would take us for another loop, and I would again turn to Sister H. We would pray and she would tell me it will get better. Year after year, time after time, this continued.

At the 10-year mark we were doing pretty good. Our business was doing well, and we seemed to be doing well as a couple and a family. But reality hit me hard in our twelfth year of marriage. It was like being hit between the eyes with a 2X4. Just when I thought we were finally over all the crazy, I discovered that I did not even know the meaning of crazy yet!

Another woman entered our lives and was trying desperately to ruin my life. She wanted my husband, my kids, my truck, my clothes, my money - she wanted my life. When I found this out, I tried to fix it. I tried everything I could, because I loved my ex-husband with all my heart and I didn't want to be known as the one that quit. I did not want a divorce. I did not want the stigma and I did not want my kids to experience the pain, confusion, or hurt that kids feel during and after a divorce.

I know some of you have experienced these same conflicting choices. Both parties must want God's help. If your spouse does not want it, and you absolutely must get out for your own protection, then God will be there for you. You can find refuge under His protective wings; just cry unto him and he will protect you, as it says in Psalms 57:1-3. I tried to spark the flames I didn't realize were dimming. I did everything I could think of. It helped for a while, but what I did not realize was that I was in a spiritual battle, and I was ill prepared for that fight.

Eph 6:12 (KJV), "For we wrestle not against flesh and blood, but against principalities, against powers, against the rulers of the darkness of this world, against spiritual wickedness in high places."

After losing almost everything, including my children and my own life, I finally discovered that the "other woman" had been summoned by witches in town who were out to destroy me and my family. My life had become a complete nightmare. The demonic attacks continued with a man, also summoned by these witches, who raped and abused me for several months. He stalked me constantly and seemed to always know where I was and what I was doing. I tried hard to get him to leave me alone, but I was in such a bad place, I did not have the strength to fight this battle by myself. I was okay if I was around my kids or friends and family. But when I was alone, this guy always showed up. I felt him watching me all the time. It was unnerving knowing I was being watched, but I could not see him. Let me just tell you, if your dog doesn't like someone, then you should sit up and listen. I felt trapped and ashamed. I felt like I could not ask for help. I felt all alone. I was being tormented daily.

Luke 22:31-32 (TPT), "Peter, my dear friend, listen to what I'm about to tell you. Satan has demanded to come and sift you like wheat and test your faith. But, I have prayed for you, Peter, that you would stay faithful to me no matter what comes. Remember this: after you have turned back to me and have been restored, make it your life mission to strengthen the faith of your brothers."

Satan's tactics are not a secret, they are as old as the struggle between Satan and mankind. It started in the Garden of Eden when he tricked Eve. He wants to isolate us from each other and from God so he can sift us as wheat. What Jesus was saying to Simon was that Satan wanted to shake him up and weaken his faith, to separate him from God. That is exactly what he did to me. He attacked everything I held dear, including my dignity and self-worth, to the point that I was afraid and ashamed to ask for help. Satan had me where he wanted me, in despair, feeling defeated and alone.

If ever you find yourself in a situation where you feel you cannot ask for help, get help, no matter how ashamed or afraid you are. Do not let Satan isolate and deceive you into believing you are worthless or too far gone. He is the father of lies – do not believe what he says. Notice the second part of this scripture, Jesus tells Simon that he has prayed for

RAISE UP

him that his faith would not fail, and that he would strengthen others after he comes through this trial. Christ will never leave us or forsake us (Heb 13:5-6). Stand strong in that knowledge and claim God's victory over Satan. Lastly, help others by sharing your testimony.

Ten months into the divorce I had discovered the spiritual source of the never-ending craziness, hurt, and despair I was experiencing. I was pinned in the corner of my own home contemplating how to end it all and get out of my mess without anyone finding out what all had happened. God showed up to rescue me. Actually, he had never left my side, I just finally reached out for help and let Him take control.

I called my cousin Karen. When she answered the phone, I was sobbing profusely. Amazingly, she had been praying for me and God had prepared her for my call. When she had calmed me down enough to talk, we prayed. Her church was in a revival and we agreed that I needed to get there right away. She lived four hours away and I was alone and being tormented. This was long before cell phones and I wasn't sure how I was going to get there alone. Karen talked with me until I was out of the house and headed down the road. Amazingly my cordless phone went with me in my car, and it worked until I was on the road away from my house. I know now that was nothing less than a miracle.

I felt the angels all around me that day. I was on a slippery slope, and I had no idea who in the world I was. Everything going on in my life was just so unbelievable – I could not comprehend it. There was a spiritual battle going on for my life and soul, and I was too weak to defend myself. Many people were praying for me, including my momma and daddy – I just did not know it at the time. Their prayers brought angels to my defense. Thank God Almighty for the power of prayer!

When I got to my cousin Karen's church, God had plans already in place to set me free and cover me with His love, grace, and mercy. I was delivered and set free from the bondage that had taken a hold of my life. I was delivered from the sin and guilt that was holding me down. Praise God Hallelujah! He set me free! I am reminded of the old hymn "He Set Me Free."

The chorus goes like this:
He set me free,
Yes, he set me free,

BEV MCCANN

He broke the bonds of prison for me,
I'm glory bound my Jesus to see.
For glory to God, he set me free.

You can be set free today! God wants to set you free through the blood He shed for you on Calvary. His sacrifice gave us the opportunity to accept His salvation, deliverance, grace, and mercy. We just need to ask Him and to give it all to Him. Even if we have wandered away from serving Him, He will still gladly accept us back and be our Lord, our Savior, and a *"friend that sticketh closer than a brother"* (Pro 18:24, KJV). God was not done with me yet and I know He's not done with you either!

Through prayer and the power of the Holy Ghost, I was able to stand up and say, "NO MORE!" I called the man who was tormenting and abusing me and boldly told him, "You will not come around me anymore and you will leave me alone." I remember him trying to make light of it all. He said, "Oh you want me back." I just about vomited right then and there (sorry for such a vivid picture). Did he just stop? No. But God gave me an inner strength to fight and be brave and hold my ground. I knew God had my back and I was somehow going to make it through with the power of the Holy Spirit and the prayers that covered me.

A few months later Dave was introduced into my life. We met in church, and I was very guarded. I told the Lord I was just fine with just God, my kids and me. But God knew that the spiritual war I was in was far from over. He knew I was going to need help fighting the battles that lay ahead. So, He sent me a knight in shining armor. As of the writing of this in 2023, Dave and I have been married 32 years. God restored me like He restored Job, giving me more than was taken. He gave me a husband that loves me to the moon and back (maybe even a little more) and so much more. He put a new song in my mouth (Psa 40:3, NSV/TPT), allowing me to minister in song and bringing forth His word.

The devil does not just stop; he must be stopped – every day. He did take a little reprieve, but only to get ready for the next attack. What he failed to see was that I was being prepared and equipped for the next battle as well. I was being covered with the Holy Spirit and suited up with the full armor of God. I grew into a deeper walk with Jesus than I had ever known. God began pouring into me knowledge of spiritual warfare. He began revealing Satan's plans and giving me the discernment to see

...ere pointed at my family and me. I was being prepared ...ld have known at the time.

...ver the next few years, attacks became relentless, but by the grace of God I was ready. There is too much to go into here, but I am in the process of putting my full testimony in a book. Suffice it to say, I faced false criminal charges, false accusations that nearly cost me the ability to make a living, faked information about my health, harassment from men in prison who thought I was seeking relationships with them, constant attacks on my kids, the untimely death of my mom, abuse of my dad that eventually led to his death, the tragic death of one of my grand-babies, and so much more. Trust me when I say, I know what it is like to have Satan try to sift you as wheat.

Looking back, I am still amazed at how hard Satan has tried to take me out. I must be a real threat to him, but thanks be unto God, I am more than a conqueror through Him that loves me (Rom 8:37-39). I am on the winning team, and you can be too!

I have learned to carry my spiritual sword with me wherever I go. It is hidden in my heart and I rehearse it daily. The Holy Spirit brings it to my remembrance at just the right time, every time. Here are just a couple scriptures I often run to. I hope you will find hope and rest in them like I do:

Psalm 94:22-23 (TPT), *"But I know that all their evil plans will boomerang back onto them. Every plot they hatch will simply seal their own doom. For you, my God, you will destroy them, giving them what they deserve. For you are my true tower of strength, my safe place, my hideout, and my true shelter."*

Psalm 18:3-4 (TLV), *"Adonai is my rock, my fortress and my deliverer. My God is my rock, in Him I take refuge, my shield, my horn of salvation, my stronghold. I called upon Adonai, (Our Lord) worthy of praise, and I was rescued from my enemies."*

In 1994, Dave took a job in Arizona and we moved out of California. Moving was one of the most difficult decisions of my life. I had never lived more than a few miles away from my parents. Now I would be 500 miles away. We affectionately refer to our nine years in Arizona as our "desert experience." In hindsight, we see how the hand of God worked in and through us during this time. We both grew tremendously under the leadership of our pastors. We gained lifelong friends and enough memories to last a lifetime. God blessed Dave's career in ways no one could have ever predicted and he birthed my songwriting and music ministry.

Since 2003, we have lived near Nashville, Tennessee. My two oldest children eventually returned to California and made lives for themselves. We adopted our youngest daughter while we were in Arizona. She is grown, has a family of her own, and lives nearby in Tennessee. After we got to Tennessee, God also blessed us with a bonus daughter. We have 7 grandkids in California that we go see as often as we can, and 10 grandkids in Tennessee. Our quiver is full and we are blessed beyond measure (remember God's restoration of Job?).

I had been in ministry since I was a teenager. As a young adult, I was a kids' church leader and kids' choir director. Satan had gotten me away from my calling for a while, but praise be to God, before we left California, He began restoring it. In Arizona, we led the church youth group. Dave served on the board of directors and ran the sound and media department, and I directed the choir. I started writing songs in 1994 and recorded my first project in 1995.

I traveled regionally around Arizona, California and Nevada with my oldest daughter who started singing when she was 15 years old. She had such an anointing when she sang. We ministered together until she graduated high school and decided to move back to California. Although she no longer sings, I know God's anointing is still on her. God will bring it back out when the time is right. She has learned to play the guitar like her grandpa (my daddy) and when she plays, it soothes my soul like David's harp soothed Saul's soul. I know her ability is a generational blessing and part of her calling.

I continued to travel as a solo artist and minister until we moved to Tennessee. God brought many new friends and pastors into my life through my travels – many of whom I am still close to and some who have gone on to receive their reward.

I remember the first song I wrote, "Not Always Thunder." I was driving a bus full of teenagers back home to Arizona from Magic Mountain in California. We had taken the youth group for a weekend of fun. As I was driving through the desert it started raining. Lightning was

RAISE UP

everywhere and the thunder was crackling all around. The words started coming to me and the tune started rolling around in my head. By the time we arrived in Kingman, Arizona, the song was complete. Eventually, it became two songs.

I remember just after releasing "Thunder", I was at a venue in Indiana and was asked to sing that song. After I got done singing, a lady came up to me and said, "how did you know?" I replied, "know what sweetie?" She proceeded to tell me that she was heading out to her car to commit suicide and when she heard that song, it stopped her in her tracks, and her life was changed forever.

God was not done with Ms. E. We became very good friends over those next several years, a friendship that continues even today. God knew what she would need years before that night, and He gave me the words to a song that helped heal her. It sends chills down my spine to think about how much God loves us. It has been over seven years since Ms. E heard that song for the first time and today, she is a changed woman. God is using her in her home church. She is teaching the little tots and God has restored her relationship with her daughter and grandkids. God restores, heals, and delivers. We only need to ask him and put our cares in his hands.

1 Chronicles 4:10 (KJV), "And Jabez called on the God of Israel, saying, Oh that thou wouldest bless me indeed, and enlarge my coast, and that thine hand might be with me, and that thou wouldest keep me from evil, that it may not grieve me! And God granted him that which he requested."

About 15 years ago, God allowed me to be pushed out of my comfort zone and into where He wanted me. I worked in real estate sales and mortgage loans for over 20 years; it was what I knew and what I was good at. When the real estate market crashed in 2008, I was left without a job and feeling rudderless. At the same time, God opened doors for me to follow my passion and His calling into the music industry. It is a long story, but suffice it to say that even though the road was rough, and not always glamorous, God protected me, connected me with wonderful Christian mentors, and took me to a new level I could have only dreamed about. I went from realtor and loan officer to music and television industry business manager, promoter, producer, and so much more. I am still humbled and amazed.

Fast forward to 2021. I was asked by my dear friend and ministry partner, Jim, to take on a new challenge. We purchased a television network, Family Friendly Entertainment (FFE on Roku), which broadcasts 24/7/365 gospel music and family friendly entertainment. This was something neither of us had any experience with and the learning curve has been steep.

Within the next three months, one of my best friends and mentors in the Christian music business asked me from his dying bed if I would please take over the business he and his wife had built over the previous 20 years - AbsolutelyGospel.com (AGM). I was hoping and praying for his recovery and that we could act like that conversation had never happened. But he said to me, "Bev, there is no one else I can trust to take it over, would you please do me this last favor, and purchase Absolutely Gospel?" I said, "let's talk when you get back home". It scared me to think he might not make it out of the hospital. A few days later, realizing he would soon be joining his wife in heaven, I called him and told him I would honor his request and purchase AGM. He passed the very next day.

Around this same time, God also connected me with the She Will Team. I did not see that one coming either. What a blessing these ladies have been to me. Not only have I been able to be a part of this wonderful ministry, but these ladies have become so very special to me. When I need encouragement, they are there. When I need prayer, they are there. When I just want to laugh and be myself, they are there too. God pushed me out of my comfort zone and gave me the opportunity to share my testimony in a way I would have never dreamed of, across the country at conferences where women come hungry for God.

In 2021, God radically enlarged my coast. At times I feel overwhelmed, but God has graciously surrounded me with a wonderful team and dear friends that I thank Him for every day. My Husband Dave, the knight in shining armor God sent to me 32 years ago, has been my rock, my confidant, my best friend, and my ever-present tech support (as he puts it, he has pulled me kicking and screaming into the 21st century of technology). As we learn and grow, I am so excited to see what all

RAISE UP

God has in store for FFE, AGM, She Will and the ministries He has me involved in.

In October 2022, a spot was discovered on my left lung. After some delays, in December, a PET scan revealed it was most likely cancer. On January 19, 2023, I went in for a biopsy surgery. The seriousness of the surgery hit me like a ton of bricks when a doctor inserted a line up a vein in my arm and all the way into my heart – just in case it stopped during the surgery!

Before I was sedated, I asked the doctors and nurses if I could pray for them. God had given me a dream a few nights before and I awoke knowing I was supposed to pray for them. They all gathered around my bed and, with Dave by my side, I prayed what God had put on my heart. Always follow the prompting of the Holy Spirit no matter how strange it may seem or how uncomfortable it may make others feel.

When I awoke, I was told what I did not want to hear. There was good news and bad news. The bad news was it was stage two cancer and the surgeon had to remove the lower lobe of my lung and the surrounding lymph nodes. I lost one-third of my lung capacity! I was devastated. How would this affect my ability to sing and speak for the Lord? How could this be? I have never smoked or even been around secondhand smoke. The good news was that the surgeon felt confident he had gotten all of the cancer out of my body.

1 Corinthians 10:13 (MSG), "No test or temptation that comes your way is beyond the course of what others have had to face. All you need to remember is that God will never let you down; he'll never let you be pushed past your limit; he'll always be there to help you come through it."

I was rocked to the core. Had I faced this news many years ago before my faith was what it is now, I would have been absolutely crushed. But God knows what we can handle, and He stands in the gap to ensure we are not tested beyond our faith. God also prepares others to be there for us. No one can get through life alone–we need each other.

Dave has constantly reminded me that God always knew this would happen and that 15-20 years ago He set in motion a series of events to protect me. It began with acid indigestion which, after years of using anti-acid pills, required surgery. The acid had gotten so bad that it was burning my vocal cords and affecting my ability to sing. Due to complications, I had two more surgeries and my doctor ordered CT scans to monitor my condition. That is how he noticed I had an aneurism in my aorta which required even more monitoring with annual CT exams. Those CT exams led to the discovery of the spot on my lung when I had no symptoms. According to my doctor, if the spot had not been discovered by the CT scans, we would not have known about the cancer until it was likely too late. By the time symptoms manifested, the diagnosis would likely have been fatal.

My struggles with acid indigestion many years ago led to the early discovery of lung cancer which literally saved my life. That realization brought new meaning to Romans 8:28 (KJV) which says, *"And we know that all things work together for good to them that love God, to them who are called according to his purpose."*

I had to come to grips with the possibility that I would no longer be able to sing and speak for the Lord. I remember telling God, "If it's your will that I never sing again like before, if you are taking my singing away because you have something else for me to do, then help me be okay. Help me understand and not struggle with the outcome." My surgeon told me not to worry, he would get me back singing in no time. I told him through my tears, "I am going to hold you to that," but I knew it wasn't up to him, it was up to God.

Through these many months of recovery, my sweet sisters at She Will have been so supportive with prayer and hugs and encouragement. They may never know how much this has meant to me, but I know that our connection was all part of God's plan. I love them all and am thankful for their love and support.

As of June 2023, my CT scan shows no signs of cancer! Praise the Lord! I was so relieved and excited. Also in June 2023, I was able to sing on the stage at the Grand 'Ole Opry during the Music City Christian Fellowship's Sunday Morning Country show. What a wonderful miracle. God is slowly restoring my stamina and lung capacity. The journey is not over yet, but I know I will make it through as long as I trust in my God, my Rock, and my Fortress to protect me.

RAISE UP

Seeing how God has been with me through all my struggles gives me the confidence to profess that He will do the same for you – you too can walk in victory. Nowhere in the Bible does God say it will be easy, but He promises victory if we put our faith and trust in Him. Your past does not determine your future—God does.

Jeremiah 29:11 (TLB), "For I know the plans I have for you, says the Lord. They are plans for good and not for evil, to give you a future and a hope."

1 Peter 5:7 (NLT), "Give all your worries and cares to God, for he cares about you."

1 Peter 1:8 (TPT), "You love him passionately although you have not seen him, but through believing in him you are saturated with an ecstatic joy, indescribably sublime and immersed in glory."

Once, when I was going through a very hard time, God gave me a song entitled, "He Will Carry You." Through the words of that song, God let me know I was not alone, that He was carrying me until I was able to walk again. Jesus loves us so much; His love is never ending.

Remember:

Isaiah 54:17 (ESV), "No weapon that is fashioned against you shall succeed, and you shall refute every tongue that rises against you in judgment. This is the heritage of the servants of the LORD and their vindication from me, declares the LORD."

Psalms 36:5 (TPT), "But you, O Lord, your mercy-seat love is limitless, reaching higher than the highest heavens. Your great faithfulness is infinite, stretching over the whole earth."

God bless you all and thank you for allowing me to share the hope of God's grace, mercy and faithfulness.

Reflect and Write Your Story
Navigating Loss, Lies & Witchcraft

Reflect:

In what way does the personal story you've just read connect with your own experiences? Is there common ground between you and the author? Explore the emotions you felt while reading. Where do those feelings stem from and how are they connected to your personal story?

RAISE UP

Writing Prompt:

Explore the concept of spiritual warfare and its presence in your life's journey. Reflect on the obstacles that have arisen along your path, considering whether you perceived them as potentially rooted in the spiritual realm. Describe how these challenges have affected your perspective and how you navigated through them.

BEV MCCANN

Scripture Connection:

Can you see where God was in this part of your story? What scriptures come to mind?

Chapter Six
Laura Anne Smith

LAURA ANNE SMITH

Laura Anne's Faith:
Exploring The Depths Beyond The Shallows

A popular proverb is, "Experience is the best teacher." As a preschool and kindergarten teacher, I provided numerous opportunities for hands-on learning and discovery. However, there is another popular quote that has merit. In the Purpose Driven Life, Rick Warren says, "While it is wise to learn from experience, it is wiser to learn from the experiences of others." How I wish I had known the Bible well enough to glean wisdom and knowledge to implement in my own life – instead of learning it the hard way.

My husband and I had grown up attending and serving in church. I had developed an honor and a reverence for God the Father, God the Son, and God the Holy Spirit. I recited prayers developed from Bible scriptures. Yet, somehow, I had missed the whole concept that *"all have sinned and fall short of the glory of God"* (Romans 3:23, NASB 1995) and that *"the wages of sin is death"* (Romans 6:23, NASB 1995). I had heard about the other half of that verse, *"But the free gift of God is eternal life in Christ Jesus our Lord."* It was as if I had accepted the blessing, without fully understanding the need for that wonderful gift of salvation. In January of 1996, we walked to the front of an arena of about 25,000 people to receive Jesus Christ as our personal Lord and Savior. Although a Christian for twenty-eight years, I had much to learn about who God is, and how to be in relationship with Him. To truly know the God of the universe, you must develop communication with Him, learn to trust Him, and begin walking with Him. Like a toddler learning to walk, I fell down– several times.

As I consider what to share in this chapter, I'm reminded of Abraham and Sarah from the Bible. In Genesis chapter twelve (NASB 1995), God calls Abram (later renamed Abraham) and Sarai (later named

RAISE UP

Sarah) to leave everything and everyone that they have ever known, setting off for an unknown location that God would later show them. God promised, *"Go… to the land which I will show you; and I will make you a great nation, and I will bless you, and make your name great; and so you shall be a blessing; and I will bless those who bless you, and the one who curses you I will curse. And in you all the families of the earth will be blessed"* (v. 1-3). Wow!! I will make you a nation! While Abram took his wife and his nephew with him, and all of the *"persons which they had acquired"* (v. 4), he couldn't bring any of his children as *"Sarai was barren; she had no child"* (Genesis 12:30, NASB 1995). In Genesis 12:7, *"The Lord appeared to Abram and said, 'To your descendants I will give this land,"* (NASB 1995). How could this be since a child had not been conceived? In Genesis 15, God promised Abram that *"one who will come forth from your own body will be your heir"* (v. 4), and continued saying, *"Now look toward the heavens and count the stars, if you are able to count them… so shall your descendants be"* (v. 5). Abram believed God, and that what he had been told would come to pass. *"Then he believed in the Lord; and He reckoned it to him as righteousness"* (Gen. 15:6, NASB 1995).

God proceeds to cut a covenant with Abram as proof that this will come to pass. Gen 15:18a says, *"On that day, the Lord made a covenant with Abram, saying, 'To your descendants I have given this land,"* (NASB 1995). God has clearly stated more than once that Abram would have a child, who the parents would be, and so on, but nothing was happening. Sarai remained barren. Abram was seventy-five years old when he was sent on this journey by the Lord. A very long ten years have passed since that day. The Bible doesn't say, but we can imagine all of the prayers and pleas that must have been offered, along with all of the disappointment and sorrow during this waiting period. Sarai must have run out of patience because she offered up her maid, Hagar, to Abram to conceive a child. She wanted this desperately for Abram. It seems as if she was trying to "help" God fulfill His promise to Abram. I also had an experience where I "helped" God to fulfill something that He had promised to me.

Shortly after our salvation experience, I began to learn what the Bible instructs about tithing. Growing up, I watched the shiny, gold offering plate pass up and down the aisles during weekly services, but I could not recall hearing what the Bible says about the tithe. In Genesis 14:20 (KJV), Abraham returned victorious in battle, and brought back "all the goods." Melchizedek, priest of God and king of Salem, spoke words of blessing over Abraham, and he paid a tenth of all of the spoils of this battle to this priest. *"Will man rob God? Yet you are robbing me. But you say, 'How have we robbed you?' In your tithes and contributions. You are cursed with a curse, for you are robbing me, the whole nation of you. Bring the full tithe into the storehouse, that there may be food in my house. And thereby put me to the test," says the Lord of hosts, "if I will not open the windows of heaven for you and pour down for you a blessing until there is no more need"* (Malachi 3:8–10, ESV). Wow! That was sobering! Who would want to steal from God?

    Like most people, my husband and I spent what we earned, and even more than we earned at times on credit. Looking at our list of monthly expenses and our checking account balance, a 10% tithe seemed impossible. We began tithing 5% of our earnings, and within six months, we were at 10%. We familiarized ourselves with the scriptures, learning how tithing helps our hearts to focus on God first. He doesn't need our money. That's not why we did it. We wanted to honor Him with the first fruits of our labor in thanksgiving.

    Additionally, we began to understand that God is Jehovah-Jireh, the God who provides. In Genesis 22, Abraham was tested by God to offer up Isaac, his only son, as a burnt offering to the Lord. When asked by Isaac where the lamb was for the burnt offering, Abraham said, *"God will provide for Himself the lamb for the burnt offering"* (Gen. 22:8, NASB 1995). In faith, Abraham continued to climb the mountain and prepare to slay his son. At the last minute, an angel of the Lord called to Abraham from heaven to say that he knew that Abraham feared God since he didn't withhold his only son. A ram appeared caught in a thicket, and was sacrificed instead of Isaac. *"Abraham called the name of that place The Lord Will Provide,"* (Genesis 22:14a, NIV).

    About a year after we began tithing, we decided that we would move from our condo to a larger house. When we listed it, our realtor cautioned that the December market was slow, and our condo was older so it might not sell right away. However, the first time they showed the condo, buyers offered us full price, which was about $25,000 more than what we had paid two years earlier. God provided the buyer and poured out blessings such that we could pay off all of our consumer debt.

When we moved into the new house, I was 29 years old, and I could hear my biological clock ticking. I told Doug that it was time to have a baby, and, by the way, I've decided that I now want to be a stay-at-home mom. God had changed my heart in that direction as I had thought that I would always work outside the home, but we had not adjusted our spending habits to prepare for the loss of my income. When Doug pointed this out, I cried. I complained to God about my husband. God seemed to speak into my mind saying, (in a way that I needed to hear it), "Get off his back. You will have a baby by the time that you are 32." Ok. Fine. There may have been some stomping feet in there somewhere. Did I trust God that this would happen when He said?

Doug said the monthly mortgage payments were too much for us to handle without my income, so we consulted our realtor. She said that as we had only lived in the house two years, and had bought the house with a VA loan (meaning we financed 104% of the cost of the house, so no equity), that we wouldn't be able to sell it without having to bring money to the closing table. She suggested that we do a "For Sale By Owner" approach, but I was afraid to try that option. Note that we did not seek God's direction, rather just proceeded to resolve the situation using logic. How I wish I had known then, *"The steps of a man are established by the LORD, And He delights in his way,"* (Psalm 37:23, NASB 1995).

When the second flyer offering to buy our home for cash arrived, we decided to do it. My older brother WISELY advised us to consult an attorney who WISELY suggested that we decline the deal. (Again, note that we consulted man, not God.) *"There is a way that seems right to a man, but its end is the way to death,"* (Proverbs 14:12 ESV).

Since we were determined to move ahead with the sale, the attorney added addendums to protect our interests if the deal went south. We moved into an apartment near my husband's job while we waited for the construction to be completed on the small house out in the country.

Next on my list: have a baby. Fortunately, we got pregnant right away. Juvenile Rheumatoid Arthritis necessitated that I take nine aspirin per day to reduce inflammation and pain. I needed to come off the medication as soon as I learned of the pregnancy, so we monitored closely. When the nurse called to confirm the pregnancy, she announced that the baby would be due on July 27th. I could hardly believe it - my baby was due to arrive the day BEFORE I turned 32! God had indeed kept His promise.

The July 11, 2022 daily devotion for In Touch Ministries reminds us that "When we remember God's faithfulness in the past, our confidence in His Word grows." Our heavenly Father is always faithful to His promises. We can be certain of this because He made them on the basis of His truthful, unchanging character (Hebrews 6:17-18). But sometimes, when our circumstances are especially difficult, we tend to forget that God is always dependable. That's why we need to pause periodically to look back over our life and see how He's provided, guided, and guarded us along the way.

I didn't remember God's past faithfulness in my life or in the Bible. I was so laser-focused on the need to resolve the financial issues so that we would be ready to have a baby by my 32nd birthday, that I misunderstood. God spoke to me as reassurance, not as if He handed me an assignment to work out on my own.

We moved into the house, and welcomed our son. Regardless of decades of working with children and families in a variety of settings, this experience was entirely different for me. The 24/7 responsibility for this small person, interrupted sleep, difficulties with breastfeeding, and physical discomfort over several weeks meant that I was not functioning at my best. The distance from family and friends left me feeling isolated and frustrated.

When our son was about 6 weeks old, we discovered that the mortgage payment on our previous house had not been paid in almost 90 days. The person who "bought" our house had placed a sign in the yard and got a buyer right away. (Remember that we had been advised to do that but didn't follow that advice out of fear.) The family living in the house paid the businessman, who then paid on the mortgage loan bearing our name - except that for 3 months now, that payment had not been made. Praise be to God that we had added the addendum from the lawyer stating that if payments failed to be made for 90 days in a row, ownership of the house then reverted to us. Only now, we had a house

RAISE UP

that we could not afford on one income, a brand-new baby, and three months of past mortgage payments that had to be paid immediately. Gulp! Long story short, the house didn't sell for over six months, so we lost about 9 months of mortgage payments plus other fees, utilities, insurance, etc. Do you remember that God said to prove Him in the tithe, that He will open the windows of heaven and pour down until there is no more need (Malachi 3:8–10 ESV)? We had continued to tithe throughout this time, and we were never late on a single mortgage payment - for either house. Our credit remained intact. God provided! Sometimes assistance came through one of our parents, and some came through Doug's 401K being cashed out without our prompting. The bottom line is that even when looking at our checkbook, we could not tell you how it happened, but God proved Himself in the tithe.

    Another lesson learned through this trial was that God sees the big picture of all the variables in our lives with a perspective that we can only gain by asking Him to reveal it to us. The month after we moved into the new house out in the country, Doug's boss gave him a job ultimatum - add travel for 50% of his time and supervise IT needs for two additional facilities, or there is the door. God wasn't surprised by this. God had also known, of course, that the businessman would end up defaulting on our house loan. God had tried to block the purchase of the new house in more than one way. We steamrolled right through the "caution" barricades because, after all, God had promised that I would have a baby by the time I was 32, and I could do the math. Surely this was the right thing to do. If only we had known how the path that we had chosen would play out. If only we had trusted in the Lord with all our hearts, and leaned not on our own understanding, He (God) would have made all of our paths straight, as He tells us in Proverbs 3:5-6 (NIV), and the potholes and detours could have been avoided.

    When Sarai offered up her maid, Hagar, to Abram so that he could conceive a child, it did not work out as she had expected. I cannot imagine the range of emotions that Sarai must have felt; however, bitterness, envy, and even shame come to mind. My situation did not work out the way that I had expected either. After eight years of marriage, we had our sweet little baby boy. I was blessed to be able to be at home with him, caring for my family in that way, but it came at a cost. We were miles from family, friends, and church. This was in 1999, so long distance calls were expensive, and texting/social media hadn't been options either. With Doug traveling half of every month, I was alone with a small child much of the time. Additionally, money was very tight. While God provided for all of our basic needs, it didn't come the way that I expected. On top of all this, every time that I would begin to heal from the negative outcomes of the house issue, we would have another court date or other trigger which brought it all to the surface again.

This wasn't fair... It wasn't supposed to be this way. I would verbally rehearse all of the wrongs, thus stirring up all of the negativity again, like a poison. Though we drove an hour each way for a brief church service, I was spiritually malnourished, feeding on unhealthy things. Unknowingly, this cultivation of unhealthy thoughts and negative emotions, yielded a harvest of bitterness, resentment, unforgiveness, and unmet expectations. The Bible warns against such things, but at this point in my journey, I was unfamiliar with what the Bible had to say. Later, I would discover warnings that could have helped, such as Hebrews 12:14-15 (ESV), *"Strive for peace with everyone, and for the holiness without which no one will see the Lord. See to it that no one fails to obtain the grace of God; that no "root of bitterness" springs up and causes trouble, and by it many become defiled."*

Through college and summers afterwards, I worked at a childcare center in West Knoxville, near my parents' home. As we continued to crawl out of the financial mess we had made, I would sometimes return to Knoxville to work during weeks that my husband traveled for work. My parents helped take care of my toddler (and me), while I earned some extra money. At the end of a long week, on a phone call with my husband, frustrations mounted until he exclaimed, "I can't do enough to please you," and I replied angrily, "No, you can't." What he said next felt like a punch in the gut, "I guess that's why some people get divorced." Wow! Talk about a big awakening! What was I doing? How did we get to this place? Convicted of my part in this turmoil, I returned home the next morning in humility and submission, desperate to give 100% of the effort required to save our marriage. Doug also apologized and agreed that divorce wasn't an option for us. He announced, "The first thing that we're going to do is to find a new church." My husband had identified the spiritual emptiness that we both felt and knew that we had to rectify that.

RAISE UP

"For his anger lasts only a moment, but his favor lasts a lifetime! Weeping may last through the night, but joy comes with the morning" (Ps. 30:5, NLT). We were desperate for that joy!

The very next day, we attended a worship service at an Assembly of God church. It was very different from the liturgical, stained glass, pipe organ, high church that we had attended for more than 30 years. As we walked to the parking lot, Doug asked what I thought about it. I replied, "It was weird, but God was there, and we'll be back."

God knew that two days later, our world would be rocked by both the tragedies of 9/11/2001, and the news of Doug's dad's diagnosis of the cancer that would end his life six years later. God knew that we needed to be shaken up, to be awakened, to be provoked to make changes to restore our marriage and overall spiritual health. God knew that we would need His love, His guidance, and His peace.

Although we had begun to work on our marriage relationship with new effort, I still harbored the unforgiveness towards the real estate crook. One Sunday morning, the pastor preached on unforgiveness. I'm sure that he spoke of the words from scripture where Jesus is asked how many times must someone forgive another (Matthew 18:21-22, Luke 17:3-4), and other such passages. All I remember is being on my knees before God, crying with mascara running down my face and my nose running while the church emptied out after the service. I felt so much lighter and free, knowing that forgiving the men involved in the real estate fraud, and forgiving ourselves, pleased God. We are to forgive as the Lord forgave us, as Colossians 3:13 tells us. Matthew 6:14-15 (NIV) seems to take it a step further in saying, *"For if you forgive other people when they sin against you, your heavenly Father will also forgive you. But if you do not forgive others their sins, your Father will not forgive your sins,"* One of the sweet, older ladies of the church came to check on me and stated that I shouldn't feel any embarrassment because anyone looking on would know that God was doing a work in my heart. That really blessed me.

After the mess that resulted from my "helping God" sell the big house so that we could downsize and afford to stay home with a baby, I was determined not to initiate a move to another house ever again. I would say, "God will have to send me a billboard, a FAX, and a memo before I will think about moving again." I had learned that lesson! I didn't want to step off the path that God had for us.

About a year and a half later, our church was reading a book that had a daily reading assignment. One afternoon, during this time, the doorbell rang. I skirted the train table, toys, and children to get to the door. The man introduced himself as our former postman. He announced that he was now selling real estate, and wondered if we would consider letting him list our house. As I shut the door, I was like Sarah who was listening at the doorway of her tent when the visitors told Abraham that when he returned at this time next year, Sarah (Abraham's wife) would have a son (Gen. 18:10 NASB 1995). Sarah laughed to herself at the seeming impossibility of it happening. I also laughed! We had tried to sell the house previously since Doug now drove 1.5 hours EACH WAY to work, 5 days per week at his new job. It would take a God-event to sell it. Frankly, we had outgrown the house so much, I couldn't even imagine getting it ready to show to prospective buyers. I called to tell my husband, thinking that we would share a laugh. Only, when I told him, I didn't hear laughter, rather he said, "Funny you should say that…" He went on to say that he was on the daily reading that encouraged parents to make changes as needed to spend quality time with their families. Since he spent 3 hours/day just driving, he wanted to get that time back to be with his boys. His reasoning was solid, and I was supportive of that decision. I knew that it was God directing our path. It certainly wasn't my idea THIS time. Trying to list the current house, locate a new house an hour and twenty minutes away, packing and coordinating all of the details with a baby and a preschooler would be a formidable task.

In the Old Testament, Gideon asked for a sign that the message given to him to deliver Israel from the oppression of the Midianites for the past seven years was from God. Gideon doubted his ability to do this, saying, *"O Lord, how shall I deliver Israel? Behold, my family is the least in Manasseh, and I am the youngest in my father's house."* (Judges 6:15, NASB 1995) Before going into battle, Gideon put out a fleece and stated that *"if there was dew on the fleece only, and it is dry on all the ground, then I will know that you will deliver Israel through me, as You have spoken,"* (Judges 6:37, NASB 1995). God made it so. The next night, Gideon asked for the opposite effect, and God also honored that

RAISE UP

request. I, too, wanted confirmation that now was the time to sell our house and move, and also that the house chosen would be the house that God wanted us to have.

My husband and I sat down and discussed what we wanted and needed in our next house. We wrote a list which included a playroom with a bay window that had a window seat, and a fireplace with a wall switch to turn on the natural gas logs. Along with the more practical number of bedrooms, bathrooms, and such, we had a list. God led me to a house currently under construction that met most of our needs. The builder showed us a lot and agreed to make a couple of changes that we thought would be a better fit for our family. We hesitated. In the meantime, God prompted me to invite a newly married couple to our house for lunch. Schedules were busy, so I hesitated to add anything else, but when the couple came, they decided to purchase our house - and they hadn't even been looking for one!! Although they had not extended an official offer yet, we met with the builder to see what our project would look like. The contract lacked two of the elements of my "fleece" related to natural gas. We prayed and felt led to go ahead and provide the earnest money and sign the contract. Following our meeting, I drove back to the lot we would be building on, and guess what? There were little yellow flags going alongside the property with the name of the natural gas company. When I told the builder that I wanted to modify the contract, he was surprised that natural gas lines were being run as they had tried to get those added to the neighborhood for years. He said, "I guess you're just getting everything you wanted, aren't you?" It hit me then that God had indeed answered my "fleece" list of house attributes. The SAME DAY, we received a signed contract for the purchase of our house in the country. He quickly rewarded our step of faith.

God's timing was perfect in so many ways. The construction process had many special moments such as when we carved a heart and Joshua 24:15 (NIV) into the concrete that had been poured for the foundation of the house. The final part of that verse says, *"But as for me and my household, we will serve the Lord."* We wrote scriptures on the 2x4s of the house, and more. It was a very special time as God demonstrated the beauty of building and moving WHEN He said, WHERE He said, and so on.

LAURA ANNE SMITH

The church we attended prior to the move has a special place in my heart. We chose to be baptized by immersion in water, dedicated our children to the Lord, were baptized in the Holy Spirit, and went through our first Dave Ramsey Financial Peace class. On one of our women's retreats, in a moment of time, I was divinely healed of Juvenile Rheumatoid Arthritis that had afflicted me for twenty-four years. I clearly remember the day that my mentor, Ms. Paulette, told me how much she enjoyed going to services at the Episcopal church because there was so much of the Word of God in the liturgy of the service. My profound response was, "Really?" I didn't have any idea that many of the prayers came from the Bible. I was Bible illiterate. I wanted my children to grow up with a solid understanding of, and familiarity with, the Holy Bible. One Sunday morning, we heard children quote Bible questions and answers, including some lengthy scripture passages, as part of the Junior Bible Quiz (JBQ) program. I knew instantly that my oldest son, Benjamin, would excel at that one day. Benjamin was age 3 at the time.

When we moved to the new house, we settled into a church that also had the JBQ program. There were 576 scripted questions and answers with about 100 direct quotations. They addressed bible doctrine and basic facts such as "Who were the first man and first woman? Adam and Eve," and "Name the 12 sons of Jacob." During our second year, we had flashcards with the question on the front and the answer and biblical reference on the back. I remember sitting on the floor of our playroom, going through the new questions at the level my son was to learn next. Question for twenty points: "What was the great sin that Ananias and Sapphira committed." Answer: "They lied to the Holy Spirit." My seven-year-old asked me who they were. My response: "I don't know." He asked: "What sin did they commit?" My response: "I don't know." The back of the card showed that this occurred in Acts 5:1-11. Always the teacher, I flipped open the Bible to read the passage. I opened the cover, located the table of contents, then scanned down until I found the page number to locate the book of Acts. I was a 39-year-old-woman, who had been in church my whole life, more than a decade since my salvation experience, and I did not have a working knowledge of where to find the book of Acts in the Bible. Talk about an awakening! Fortunately, I have always been a learner, so instead of getting discouraged, I began to learn alongside my sons.

RAISE UP

During our four years in this program, we had teaching opportunities to expand and reinforce the learning of Bible concepts, in addition to all of the recitation. In 2007, my oldest was seven-years-old during the summer that we assisted with the care of my father-in-law who was receiving hospice care for terminal cancer. I later learned that I was experiencing an early menopause. Not a good combination. One day, when I snapped at my son, I immediately apologized for my curtness. I explained feeling very anxious about Grandad. He quoted to me, *"Do not be anxious about anything, but in everything, by prayer and petition, with thanksgiving, present your requests to God. And the peace of God, which transcends all understanding, will guard your hearts and your minds in Christ Jesus,"* (Phil. 4:6-7, NIV 1984). Wow! How do you respond to that? He was right! I needed to trust God and walk in His peace. After I got past the astonishment of the proper application of the verse needed in that moment, I realized how powerful that was and wanted to learn more scripture myself.

Through homeschooling, we were introduced to the National Bible Bee which took our Bible memory program to a whole new level. The first year my oldest participated in the program, his age division had to memorize 500 scripture verses by citation (such as Genesis 1:1-15… without giving them a question prompt first). They also studied the book of Colossians in depth. I clearly remember thinking that there's no way that he can do this in just over two months! It took him two years to memorize the 576 questions and answers in JBQ.

Fortunately, the Lord helped me to withhold my doubts. We had an opportunity to study a few times with others also studying in this program. Another child asked him if he planned to memorize the entire list of verses. She said that she did it last year and planned to do it this year. The young lady seated behind us was in the older division and said that she planned to memorize all 800 of her verses that summer. He looked at first one girl and then the other, nodded once thoughtfully, and in his mind, it was done. He was going to do this! I say that to mention the power of being in community with others who have similar goals and work on it together. The following year, the program changed and added an additional 200 verses to be memorized in about two months and to study a second book of the Bible before the national competition. 700

verses! We also added reading Bible commentary on the Bible books and worked through the Precept Ministries adult level studies alongside the Bible Bee materials.

I learned the importance of looking up the definitions of words in Webster's Dictionary to make sure that I understood what the words meant in English before cross-referencing and possibly looking at the Greek. Colossians 3:8 says *"But now you also, put them all aside: anger, wrath, malice, slander, and abusive speech from your mouth"* (NASB 1995). In the margin of my Bible today are brief definitions of what each of those mean, causing me to pause and fully think through their meanings as I evaluate if I am feeding any of those negative feelings. I don't want to return to that place of bitterness and anger. God inspired every word that the Bible writers penned, so if you see words that appear to have similar meanings, dig in and identify the differences. They must have significance. *"All Scripture is inspired by God and beneficial for teaching, for rebuke, for correction, for training in righteousness;"* (2 Tim. 3:16, NASB).

The Lord has often used me to pray with and for people. What is more powerful than praying God's Word over the situation? Hebrews 4:12 says, *"For the word of God is living and active, and sharper than any two-edged sword, even penetrating as far as the division of soul and spirit, of both joints and marrow, and able to judge the thoughts and intentions of the heart,"* (NASB). Even though I do not have the gift of precise scripture recitation that my sons have developed, phrases and quotes from God's word will come into my mind during situations or be spoken into prayers. I recently had an adult woman tell me that when she had strayed off the path into drugs, she would sometimes hear the JBQ quotes in her mind that she had learned as a child, and it helped her return to the Lord. Isaiah 55:11 speaks to the power of God's word, *"So will My word be which goes out of My mouth; It will not return to Me void (useless, without result), Without accomplishing what I desire, And without succeeding in the matter for which I sent it,"* (Isaiah 55:11, Amp).

I studied about the names of God to learn the character of God. What does God say about Himself? Who is He? Can we trust Him to provide (remember Jehovah-Jireh)?

RAISE UP

It is essential to know God's character and what He says in His word, lest you may be deceived. Jesus warns of this in Matthew 24:4. In Colossians 2:4 (NASB), Paul writes, *"I say this so that no one will deceive you with persuasive arguments,"* The past few years have seen unprecedented changes in our country, most moving further away from being one nation under (a Judeo-Christian) God. Change begins with each of us, in our hearts, as the Holy Spirit leads us to stand up for the truth of God's Word in our homes, in our schools, in the workplace, in the larger community, and in the country.

On May 28, 2023, Dr. Raleigh Washington, President and CEO of Awakening The Voice of Truth, spoke at World Outreach Church, Murfreesboro, TN. He proclaimed that each of us has the power to destroy false narratives if you are in Christ Jesus. He said that the word "false" means lie which comes from the father of lies/the devil (John 8:44). When tempted by Satan, Jesus destroyed a lie with the truth. Dr. Washington urges us to see, evaluate, understand, and interpret everything through the Word of God. Be unafraid to USE the word of God. To do that, we must know the word of God. Read it. Study it. Know it. Live it.

No matter where you are on your journey as a follower of Jesus Christ–It's not too late! All of us can continually learn, grow, be and become! With Abraham and Sarah, it was about 14 years after the birth of the child by Hagar that Sarah, age 90, gave birth to baby Isaac. Abraham was 100 years old. Genesis 21:1 says, *"Then the Lord took note of Sarah as He has said, and the Lord did for Sarah as He had promised"* (NASB 1995). God did what He said He would do. *"Is anything too difficult for the Lord?"* (Gen. 18:14a, NASB 1995). A note in the margin of my Bible says, "God fulfilled His promise in such a way that you knew that it was God." There was no doubt in Sarah's or anyone else's mind that this was a God-event.

I have also experienced unmistakable God-events. Romans 8:28 says, *"And we know that God causes all things to work together for good to those who love God, to those who are called according to His purpose,"* (NASB 1995). The Amplified version of the Bible adds words and phrases to help illuminate concepts. It says, *"And we know [with great confidence] that God [who is deeply concerned about us] causes all things to work together [as a plan] for good for those who love God, to those who are called according to His plan and purpose,"* (AMP 2015). My hope as a Christian and as a teacher is that you will love God and learn more about Him through His word, the Bible, and then live it out in your lives.

Reflect and Write Your Story
Exploring The Depths Beyond The Shallows

Reflect:

In what way does the personal story you've just read connect with your own experiences? Is there common ground between you and the author? Explore the emotions you felt while reading. Where do those feelings stem from and how are they connected to your personal story?

LAURA ANNE SMITH

Writing Prompt:

Reflect on the scriptures that have anchored you through life's ups and downs. Describe the promises from God's word that you have personally witnessed coming to fruition in your journey. Delve into the impact of these fulfilled promises on your faith and outlook.

RAISE UP

Scripture Connection:

Can you see where God was in this part of your story? What scriptures come to mind?

Chapter Seven
Thresa Lawson

Thresa's Redemption:
Overcoming The Unexpected

We're all guilty. We plan and expect the perfect life. If we come from this family, go to this school, avoid bad habits, do good to people, then we can have the perfect, well- planned life. Why shouldn't we? Living in America we learn to dream the impossible. Lasso the moon and reach for the stars!

Then the unexpected happens. Something we didn't plan for occurs, like an illness, divorce, death, a child on drugs, layoffs, financial setbacks or ruin. The list is endless and it is generally more than one major stressor that hits at any given time. Daily we hear heartbreaking stories of lives that didn't go as planned.

Everyone will, at one time or another in their life, experience "the unexpected." So how do you raise up after the unexpected? I learned through personal experiences that we may not have the answers to all our questions, but we know "the answer." The oft quoted phrase by Charles Spurgeon is applicable here. "God is too good to be unkind and He is too wise to be mistaken. And when we cannot trace His hand, we must trust His heart." The meaning is, we may not always understand the circumstances in life, but we can trust God is with us. He is intimate with every detail of our life and, if we allow Him, He can help us rise above the unwanted, unexpected circumstances.

During my sophomore year, I met a young man on the track team. We saw each other every day while training and began running together. He was dark-haired with deep chocolate eyes, a rich tan, and high cheekbones, displaying an obvious Native American heritage. I enjoyed our blossoming friendship and certainly loved the attention he gave. We eventually started dating. At sixteen, I was more enamored with the romantic notions of being in love, rather than understanding what true love and a meaningful relationship were about. I had been bullied during my junior high years, so to have both athletic recognition at last and the attention of a handsome young man, it's no surprise I was swooning.

He wasn't a Christian when I met him, but I still invited him to church. To please me, he agreed, and would faithfully attend church, seeming to support my relationship with Jesus wholeheartedly. It wasn't long before I introduced him to my family, giddy with excitement over this new adventure in my life. He would drive me home from practice and we would sit in the car for hours talking. We didn't "go out" much, as we didn't have the extra funds, so most of our time together was spent at my house. Within six months of dating, we were "in love," so we made plans to marry.

In the early 1970s, in the small Southern town where I grew up, it was not uncommon for a girl to marry young. I wasn't pregnant. I was still a virgin. And I wasn't trying to get away from home. We were both so young and naïve that it just seemed like the right thing to do. If I'm honest, I think I was the one who pushed the idea of getting married more than anyone. My parents were guarded but were under the impetus of, *"it's better to marry than to burn with passion"* (I Corinthians 7:9, NIV).

Truth be told, I distinctly remember having second thoughts about getting married, but would brush them away as wedding jitters. Though I felt we were rushing things, my desire to be wanted, loved, and married outweighed any apprehension. I'd already achieved my dream of athletic recognition, but maybe I felt this marriage would lock in genuine acceptance and would be the icing on the cake. Honestly, all I can rationalize now is we were young and dumb and made a decision that many times caused me to ask, "Why in the world did I do that?" I won't even try to explain what he was feeling or thinking, but perhaps the desire for conquest overrode any notions of wisdom and sanity.

So, we moved forward with plans for a wedding, though the unsettling in my spirit continued. I remember one beautiful, balmy afternoon that the Holy Spirit spoke to me. I was walking in our backyard by the detached garage where my dad operated his third job of working on cars in the evenings. As clearly as I have ever heard anything, I heard the Spirit of the Lord admonish me not to get married. The words were so clear and so firm I froze in my tracks. To this day I can still smell the

RAISE UP

mixture of oil, grease, and gasoline through the garage's open window, but at that moment, it was like I was covered in a cloud, blinded by an otherworldly fog. I didn't heed the warning, though with all my heart I wish I had.

    A few months shy of my seventeenth birthday, we were married in the little church we attended. There was no expensive wedding dress. No elaborate flowers. My bouquet was a hastily prepared "do it yourself" creation. The only thing I remember is that my wedding day felt just like any other day. Mom made her delicious, spicy, sloppy joes, and that was the meal before the wedding. There was no rehearsal. No fanfare. Just a small gathering of our parents and a few friends. My husband told me later that he seriously contemplated running out the back door before entering the sanctuary.

    After our first week of marriage, we were already forced to part ways. He had joined the Army and was to be stationed at Fort Riley, Kansas. When I drove him to the bus station and watched him jump on the bus to head to basic training, I knew this was not how I'd pictured married life. No picket fence and apple pies and all the trappings of an American dream. Just a confused teenage bride caught between childhood and the stark realities of becoming an adult. I stayed with my parents to finish up my junior year of high school, then packed up and moved to Kansas as well, to join my husband.

    It didn't take long for me to realize not all homes were like the one where I was raised. The school of hard knocks was about to begin. And I mean that in more ways than one.

    Do you ever wish life could be like a fairy tale? You meet and marry the love of your dreams, have two beautiful, compliant, perfect children, then live debt free in a beautiful home with two cars, a picket fence, and endless days of wedded bliss? Who wouldn't?

    As a little girl, I felt I had the perfect family as a model of what could be. Raised in a wonderful, godly, Christian home, I never heard my parents argue - the operative word being "heard." I learned many years later that if they were miffed at one another, they would take a car ride so the little ears in the house wouldn't hear the argument. That aside, it was the perfect setting for a fairy tale.

    My mother was a stay-at-home mom who cooked three meals a day, which we actually sat down to eat together, as opposed to modern families. My parents prayed together, took us to church — in one car — and are still married today after sixty-five years. By today's standards, we were unique.

My heritage goes beyond my parents. My grandparents were exemplary in their Christian walk and witness. Grandma made sure we all knew the importance of family. As far as she was concerned, no stronger bond or commitment existed. We would regularly meet at my grandparents' home for food, fun, and fellowship. The "family get-togethers," as they are fondly remembered, resembled a church service. My dad was the second of eight children, and each child had at least two children of their own. So, our family gatherings were the size of most small churches. Our worship style was Pentecostal with Southern country flair. Someone would sing, someone would share a testimony, and someone else would share their musical talents on an instrument. God was the very essence of our family life. We loved, laughed, fought, made up, and cared deeply for one another. Such was life in the perceivably (perhaps deceivingly) happy world in which I developed and matured. Because of my heritage, I grew up believing all families loved each other, all marriages were good, and the same couple stayed together for life.

So, when I got married, I naively thought all homes were like my family. I had the perfect little marriage and home planned out. I was in love, as much as a sixteen-year-old can be, and people in love get married. I didn't ask God or others what they thought of my plan. There were many people who expressed doubt that my marriage would last, but were summarily dismissed as naysayers. Quickly, however, my little wall of shelter came crumbling down.

Our first argument started when he got angry while watching a football game on television. It was a beautiful fall afternoon, and I was preparing lunch after arriving home from church. There I was, happy little Suzy homemaker, busily cooking a wonderful meal for my husband, when every bit of peace in that trailer exploded like a bomb, as if the fragments of our home were falling all around me. Never in my life had I ever seen anyone become so angry. I told him to stop. Not a good idea. He blew up, jumping to his feet and cursing me with a string of profanity so shocking I was left bewildered. Surely, he didn't realize what he was saying. But my rebuke was like throwing gas on an already raging fire. He

RAISE UP

grabbed the family Bible lying on the coffee table and began ripping out the pages, one by one. "Stop!" I screamed, tears of shock streaming down my face. With eyes wild, he picked up the coffee table and smashed it on the ground. All the while I just stood there speechless, baffled how such a pointless thing as a football game could thrust him into such a state. He'd become a lunatic. A madman bent on destroying our little home. All I could think to do was try to settle him down.

With little to no experience in conflict resolution, much less dealing with a lunatic, I did the first thing that came to mind. I dashed to the little broom closet beside the kitchen and grabbed the broom. With adrenaline coursing through my veins, and clearly clouding my better judgment, I lifted my make-shift weapon with all my might and promptly swatted his behind. This wasn't the smartest move. If I thought he was angry before, things now erupted to a stratospheric level. Like a grizzly bear poked in the ribs, he flew into an even wilder rage and came at me with teeth bared, spewing forth a string of adjectives so profane my eyes filled with even more tears. But my clear hurt did me no favors. He picked me up like a toy and threw me against the wall. A searing pain shot through my back right as my head whiplashed into the wall with a sickening thud. I can still remember thinking as I was sliding down the wall, my vision blurred from tears and agony, "What in the world is going on? Who is this person? I am looking at a madman!" I passed out before hitting the floor.

When I came to, he was leaning over me, his expression a mask of fear and dread. He'd clearly come to his senses enough to realize what he'd done. But when he realized I was alive, he didn't apologize. He didn't ask if I was hurt. He just laughed nervously and turned away to pick up the evidence of his tirade. Dazed, I numbly walked back to the kitchen in a state of utter shock.

That day was just a taste of what was to come. A foreboding reminder that my new home was definitely not going to be the wonderful, peaceful, Christian home of my upbringing. Still, as I'd heard from my parents so many times before, once the "I dos" are spoken, it's till death do us part. I wouldn't run, despite how fear, guilt, uncertainty, sadness, and regret became my constant companions and the escapades of angry, abusive outbursts continued. I had heard the scriptural admonition not to marry an unbeliever, but naively thought it would be different for me. I was surely the exception. Oh, the naïveté of youth!

Regardless of how bad it got at the time; I was determined not to complain to my family. I had chosen this path, and I was going to try to make the best of it, though my expectations of the perfect Christian home were quickly crumbling at my feet. I went from living with a fantastic family and wonderful home life to what felt like solitary confinement in a single-wide trailer. Instead of excelling in varsity volleyball and track and being a member of the student council, I had become a poor, depressed housewife living behind a tavern without a telephone or even a car. This was no little girl's dream.

Despite my devastating wake-up call, I still thought I could magically turn our home into the illusion of my childhood dreams. The only thing I knew to do was fast and pray for my husband and our home. I did, fervently, but it seemed the more I prayed, the worse he became. He began to drink heavily and stay out all night partying with his soldier friends from the base. Eventually, drugs entered the picture and things grew exponentially worse. We were living in two different worlds, with opposite moral codes. There were many explosive episodes linked to my husband's addictions and our collective immaturity. I learned to despise drugs and alcohol and their destructive effects.

Even an ordinary trip to the grocery store could leave me feeling humiliated and weeping. A simple difference of opinion could turn into a barrage of verbal darts, each one sending a message of worthlessness and hopelessness. I would feel so embarrassed standing in the canned goods aisle. Mascara streaked down my crimson face, making me look and feel like a deflated balloon.

During that first year of marriage, I learned that life's struggles can't be resolved in a day and that broken hearts need more than glue to be restored. The physical bruises may heal, but the emotional and mental wounds take much longer to put back together. I was struggling to make sense of the abuse, with no mentor or friend to walk me through it all. It was a difficult time, coming to grips with the culture shock of living with an unbeliever, and I was totally unprepared for the devastation that abuse plays on one's mind. The mental and emotional fragments were adding up.

RAISE UP

    I felt like I was being punished by God for some unknown word or deed. I didn't understand what I had done to deserve a home so different from the one I had hoped and dreamed about. In my mind, I didn't deserve the pain I was now experiencing.

    Have you ever felt mad at God? That almost sounds sacrilegious, but if we are honest, we have all sensed that emotion at one time or another. You put your faith, trust, and confidence in God, you believe He will answer or perform in a certain way, and, alas, your hopes are dashed. So, you end up being angry at God. I was perplexed and angry that a loving God would allow me to experience this suffering. I was angry that I felt trapped in a hopeless situation.

    However, the greatest emotional wound I suffered during that time was rejection. That one emotion left me feeling completely broken and hopeless of repair. Rejection hits like a well-placed punch in the pit of your stomach. My husband was unfaithful to our marriage vows and seemed indifferent to the devastating emotional effects it had on me.

    Isn't it amazing how another person can hurt you so badly that everything you view afterwards is tainted by the pain inflicted? I felt like my emotions were nothing more than shards of pain lying on the floor. My emotions at that time reminded me of a time my grandmother's favorite lamp was lying broken into pieces on the floor.

    When I was a young girl I would frequently visit my grandmother. One morning, I paid her an early morning visit. Visits to grandma were usually quite uplifting, with homemade biscuits and gravy, and talk of gardening and family. However, this particular morning, I found her sitting on the sofa crying. What could cause this much sadness so early in the morning? My cousins. They were four years old and full of energy and, yes, mischief. This particular morning the two "energized bunnies" were testing the limits by fighting, biting each other and getting into trouble. Soon, they began fighting over breakfast and took the fight into the living room where they inadvertently bumped into a lamp that held great sentimental value for grandma. The lamp toppled and landed in pieces on the floor. The crash drew grandma's attention from the stove to the living room where she saw the lamp lying broken on the floor.

    Bewildered, she knelt beside the broken pieces and began to pick them up one by one. The poor little cads stood by helpless as grandma burst into tears. That is when I came in and found her sitting on the sofa with her head in her hands crying.

My uncle, father to one of the guilty parties, came in shortly and learned what had happened. It was so precious to watch him go straight to his mother and put his arms around her and say, "It's O.K, Momma. I'll fix it." He got the glue, and knelt beside the broken lamp and spent several hours very carefully and tediously putting the lamp back together. Later, grandma recalled the story for another family member. Instead of applauding the beautiful work my uncle did in repairing the special lamp, she spoke most appreciatively of him putting his arms around her and comforting her and promising to "fix it."

When I was living at home with mom and dad, I felt cherished, accepted, and wanted. No matter what I endured during the day, there was a warm meal and hug waiting for me when I arrived home. Now, there was no one waiting for me inside that empty trailer. No one knew the pain I was experiencing. There were no loving arms to console me or tender words to speak comfort to my wounded spirit, letting me know that they would "fix it." I was miserable, and it felt like I cried all the time.

That is when I knew that my heavenly Father saw my pain and tears, and most of all he cared. One day, as I was changing my little boy's diaper, heavy tears poured from my eyes. Laying the baby back in the bed, I spoke candidly to the Lord, "I feel like all I do is cry and pray." Then the most beautiful scene unfolded. It seemed as if the wall beyond the baby bed faded, and a voice spoke to me, saying, "It was for those tears that I died." I knew then the Lord was telling me He was acquainted with grief and that He would bear my sorrow.

"Surely He has borne our griefs (sicknesses, weaknesses, and distresses), and carried our sorrows and pain." (Isaiah 53:4, Amplified Bible)

The next Sunday in church, the Lord confirmed He was with me and was very aware of my pain. God always makes a way for His children in the unexpected seasons. He does come, He does share our sorrows and He is always there for us. No situation is too difficult for

RAISE UP

Him, no heart beyond repair, and no pain too great for Him to mend. Even when it seems totally hopeless, He is there.

Our already shaky marriage was about to be shaken to its foundation. We were stationed at Fort Carson, Colorado, but we did not have any money or a place to live. So, with our two children, we moved into a cheap one-star, musty smelling motel room with a little kitchenette. Looking at the bed, I wondered if the rumpled, dingy sheets had even been cleaned. We eked out an existence week by week with barely enough to pay for the motel. There was nothing left for groceries, so I bought a bag of self-rising flour and made flapjacks for us to eat. I stayed in that little room with the two children day and night. My husband would go to the base, in the only vehicle we owned, where he was provided for, while the children and I fended for ourselves.

The furnishings were meager, with a bed and one straight-back chair that I pulled up to a small table. I cooked our flapjacks over a little two-burner stovetop. The room had a small alcove with a window. I pulled the table and chair over by the window, and this became my place of meditation and study. For hours on end, I would sit at that little table with my Bible, notepad, and pencils. I would push play on my little tape recorder, read a bit, jot down some notes, then lean back in my chair and look out the window at the beautiful mountains. The backdrop for my meditation and study time was a gift from God. The view was spectacular and just looking at the majestic snow-capped mountains was a healing balm like no other.

I guess by human standards, I should have gone mad. It's amazing what you do when you must survive. There was just so much "God" in that small room, I thought less and less of what we lacked. I only had one tape to listen to, and it was a Southern Gospel family called the Hemphills. I would play that one tape all day long as I read the Bible and prayed or played with the children. My favorite song was "Master of the Wind."

When I look back on that time of homelessness, I don't grimace or get sad, but rather feel a deep sense of joy thinking about the unfailing love of God. My little prison of a hotel room became a palace of His presence, and I, too, could sing songs of worship. It's amazing what you really need for happiness.

THRESA LAWSON

Our marriage did not survive. Ideally, it would have been great if we could have had a beautiful marriage with no problems. I guess we were just too young and from two different worlds. He joined the Army barely out of his teens, and the temptations and peer pressure were just too much. He struggled with addictions that millions struggle with. Unfortunately, the lifestyle associated with addictions also affects loved ones. God indeed turned the situation with me and my ex into something good, and I believe He wants to do the same for all who will allow him to heal their brokenness.

This story has a happy ending. More than happy. Vance was a gift from God and our life together over the past several decades has been a blessing too wonderful to describe. No life is perfect and without difficulties. But my new marriage has brought such love and healing not only for myself but for my kids as well.

However, one of the unwanted, lasting effects of my first marriage and ensuing divorce was bitterness. It started as anger, then progressed to hate, and finally turned into a full-blown bitter root of resentment. I was a Christian, actively serving God to the best of my ability and faithful to church, but through various circumstances that continued, I became entrenched in bitterness. There is nothing more hideous than an unforgiving, embittered spirit. Thankfully, God would not tolerate that spirit in me.

I was in Missouri picking up my daughter's car from my family's body shop. As I was sitting in the waiting room of the shop waiting for the last details to be completed on her car, the shop door opened and in walked the postman. I glanced up from the magazine I was perusing, smiled, and said, "Hi." He glanced my way and replied the same. After the postman laid the mail down on the counter and walked out, I decided I needed to use the restroom. I was thinking to myself, "That guy sure looks familiar." It had been fifteen years since I had seen my ex-husband. While I was in the restroom, the postman, who was my ex-husband, walked back into the shop and approached my dad and asked if he could talk to me. My dad was hesitant but replied that it was my decision. When I walked out of the restroom, my dad pulled me aside and told me that my ex-husband wanted to talk to me.

We sat down in the waiting room, and he asked how I was doing. I answered the question and asked how he was doing as well. What proved so astounding about that moment was not the fact that I was having a conversation with my past abuser, but that I had no hatred, no bitterness, and no fear. I searched my heart and felt only peace. I told him how each one of the children were doing. He said he was very grateful for Vance being such a good father to the children. I didn't sense his old jealousy. I didn't know the state of his soul, or if he'd ever come to faith. But our peaceful conversation was proof enough that the past was in the past. Our collective pain was insurmountable. His offenses beyond human pardon. But by God's grace, I knew I had forgiven him and moved on. And I could only hope that this man before me could experience the same freedom.

    We chatted a little more, then said goodbye. As I watched him leave, my dad quickly walked over to where I was and put his arms around me. "Sis," he said. "Are you OK?" It was clear he was recalling all the pain I'd endured at the hands of the man who had just left his shop. With supernatural calm, I answered. "Yeah dad, I'm fine." It was amazing to see the work God had done in my heart. The feelings of hurt, betrayal, unforgiveness, and bitterness were gone. All the wounds of the past had been healed.

    A few minutes later, my ex walked back through the door, looked at me, and asked, "Thresa, can I talk to you outside for just a sec?" My dad stood up, and I looked over at him and said, "It's OK, Dad." I smiled and walked outside, with my dad peeking out the window, wondering what more he had to say.

    He looked at me earnestly and said, "Thresa, I want to ask your forgiveness for all the pain I've caused you and for not being a good husband." To say I was shocked is an understatement. But even as he said these words, finally humbling himself and saying he was sorry, I realized something miraculous and surprising. Now that I'd received what I'd so desperately wanted from him, I realized I didn't need him to say it anymore. With tears in my eyes, I reciprocated and asked for his forgiveness as well. God had so completely healed my heart and allowed me to forgive him even before he asked for it. At that moment, I was overwhelmed with the absolute wonder of Jesus.

    The unexpected healing of our broken places doesn't mean that our scars are always healed. In fact, that may not be a bad thing. Scar tissue is stronger than ordinary skin because of the amount of fiber cells needed. I think the same is true emotionally. As noted earlier, I had many experiences that could have done significant damage physically, mentally, and emotionally. Instead, by allowing Jesus into those times, the place of woundedness became a stronger place and a solid reminder of God's faithfulness.

It reminds me of the wounds Jesus suffered as He was wounded for our transgressions and bruised for our iniquities. Those scars on His hands and feet are a reminder, not of the pain, but of the victory received! Remember, no matter what life brings, Jesus loves you more than you can imagine and will hold you close and give you sufficient grace no matter what. Jacob walked with a limp after his midnight wrestling match where God touched his hip socket and Jacob's hip was put out of joint. What did he have to say about the encounter? *"So, Jacob called the name of the place Peniel, saying, "For I have seen God face to face, and yet my life has been delivered* (Gen 32:30, NKJV). I believe God is never closer than when we experience the unexpected circumstances of life - and we will. No one is exempt from "life." The key is to not allow the unexpected circumstances to overwhelm or destroy us. I believe the parable of the old donkey and farmer is applicable here:

One day a farmer's donkey fell into an abandoned well. Terrified, the animal cried for hours as the farmer tried to figure out what to do. Finally, he decided the animal was old and impossible to retrieve. He realized the well needed to be filled to prevent future losses. So he invited all his neighbors to help him.

They all grabbed shovels and began to throw dirt into the well. At first, when the donkey realized he was being buried alive, he cried horribly. Then, to everyone's shock, the donkey quieted down. A few shovel loads later, the farmer looked down the well and was astonished at what he saw. With each shovel of dirt that hit the donkey's back, the donkey would shake it off and take a step up.

As the farmer and his neighbors continued to throw dirt on top of the animal, he would shake it off and take another step up. Soon everyone was amazed as the donkey stepped up over the edge of the

RAISE UP

well and happily trotted off! (Farmer's Donkey. (n.d.). WisdomShare. Retrieved June 28, 2023 from https://wisdomshare.com/stories/farmers-donkey/)

The goal of the enemy of our soul is to bury us. I love the analogy, shake off the dirt and raise up! We must raise up after the unexpected. Zig Zigler, a noted motivational speaker, summed it up best: "It's not what happens to you that determines how far you will go in life; it is how you handle what happens to you."

Reflect and Write Your Story
Overcoming The Unexpected

Reflect:

In what way does the personal story you've just read connect with your own experiences? Is there common ground between you and the author? Explore the emotions you felt while reading. Where do those feelings stem from and how are they connected to your personal story?

RAISE UP

Writing Prompt:

Examine a significant crisis of belief you've faced in your RAISE UP story. Describe how you navigated through this period of doubt or uncertainty. Did you seek guidance from a mentor or a pastor? Explore the insights gained and the impact of this experience on your beliefs and personal growth.

THRESA LAWSON

Scripture Connection:
Can you see where God was in this part of your story? Do any scriptures come to mind?

Chapter Eight
Tammy Manning

Tammy's Unveiling:
Addressing Generational Sin

Allow me to paint the backdrop: Once upon my younger years, well, my teenage ones to be precise, the journey commenced during my childhood and within the pages of this chapter the narrative unfolds, guiding you through my emotional journey until I reach my late twenties.

I watched. I observed. I heard. My family's whole world changed in what seemed like the blink of an eye. I was not the child abused, but the bi-product of the family left in shattered pieces, like glass shards. The devil came in and attacked my family.

My family unit was like something out of a 50s sitcom. We were a happy, wholesome family until, one day, the lies of Satan were exposed by the light of God. Sounds perfect, huh?

I mean, the Light of Truth is what we want until it affects our image and has the potential to bring everything out, to expose every sin anyone has ever committed. The truth will expose what we really are and our pasts may not line up with our present.

So, nowadays, we're all about sharing every little thing in our culture, right? I mean, social media is full of picture-perfect posts and all that. But back in the 50s, before the whole social media craze, we had these closets. Yeah, you heard me right, closets. And their main gig? Well, it was to stash away all the stuff nobody really needed to know about. Like, those things just stayed locked up tight in there. Keep those skeletons in there! Throw away the key.

The closet door slung open and the skeletons released. My teenage self became a byproduct of them. The word byproduct means a result of another's actions, often unseen and/or unintended.

I was hurt. Everything that I knew was gone. Family suppers at my grandparents. GONE. Sitting in church on the third pew from the

RAISE UP

front, second section from the left with my grandparents. GONE. Laughter in my home was replaced with silence, pain, and anger. Safety was replaced with confusion. Large Family Unit split up, isolated. I did not know where my cousins were or if they were okay. I would ask and be told they are good and safe. Out of sight, out of mind, right? No, in my head, it was more confusion. A life of kumbaya. GONE!

I was a child. I did not see or know that the family head, my grandfather, was a deacon with a very dark past. He led a life Monday-Saturday one way, but wore a suit and carried a Bible on Sundays. This man left a line of damage to his children, and they, in turn, made unhealthy damaging choices. They pushed past their damage and pain and anger prevailed as they parented. This is where generational curses are birthed. The glass shards are stepped on for centuries to come. We have all heard it: hurting people hurt people. I believe none of it was intended to hurt others, just a way of life that they had learned by building walls, ignoring the trauma, hoping to be loved by anything, and sometimes letting their emotions go to anger as they had seen their whole life.

This is my story - not the stories of the damage to my aunts, uncles, parents, or cousins, but told from my heart and sight. My memories. My walls. My defenses. My sins. My victory. Jesus' Freedom. God's grace. The Holy Spirit's infiltration in my life.

I have loved Jesus since I can remember. I love sitting with Him and talking to Him. Some kids have imaginary friends. I had nature, long walks, forts in the forest, "raw land in Texas' backyard," and talks with the Creator. I have loved being alone and talking to God for as long as I can remember. I heard Him. We talked for hours, and I would get lost in fantasy with Him. He was always my escape.

My grandparents were solid Christians in the eyes of a child. They attended church. They also sent the Pastor to our house all the time. (INSERT LOL). My Daddy would have words with the Pastor, which never ended well. I felt sorry for the Pastor. He was just trying to get them to come to church. Truthfully, I feared the Pastor. He always yelled in church and banged his fist on the pulpit. He was passionate about keeping people out of hell. I did love Sunday School, working in the Nursery, and holding the babies.

TAMMY MANNING

I was a bus kid. My parents would not get up and take me to church, but the bus showed up every week. I would get my sisters ready, and on the bus, we would go. That bus was a lifeline for me. The Church of Christ picked us up on Wednesdays and First Baptist got us on Sundays. I loved the community aspect that the church provided. These were the best days of my life.

I was ten years old when I accepted Christ. I can take you to the spot. It was in the Fellowship Hall, in the back of the First Baptist Church, around the middle of the room to the left. We had a revival that week, and I remember the moment when I could no longer deny what I was feeling and gave my life to Jesus. Next was baptism; I was on cloud NINE. However, I was disappointed quickly with anything in my life that revolved around religion.

The Pastor came to my house to talk to my parents. My dad said that I could not be baptized and that they would not push religion on me. He never asked me; he just said I was too young to make this decision. As a teenager, I became mouthy and was in trouble a lot, which meant that I would get grounded A LOT! My dad started grounding me from church as He said it was the only thing I cared about losing.

I had in my life this melting pot of what Christianity looked like. My parents did not represent it at all in our home. Now, please understand they were not bad parents. They were excellent parents. They loved us. They protected us. They showed me what marriage should be. Their love for each other was amazing. What my dad was doing, was protecting me from something that had hurt him, damaged him. Religion. My Papa was all my dad knew of God or Jesus. He was a by-product of my grandparents' wanting to save their image in the church. I mean, he was a deacon, and as a deacon, your kids must be in the right standing or you lose that status. My dad hated Church and Religion. My parents played with us, taught us how to raise animals, and took us camping. They did all the things. They taught us how to be a strong family unit. They also even spent Sundays at our grandparent's house for family meals. It was the perfect family; however, we never discussed Jesus, God, or Church.

One day, our whole world crumbled. The family unit (from Grandparents down to the bottom of the family tree) was severed by one

RAISE UP

man's sin, or so we thought. I know today that the devil comes in and can affect one person, but sin damages everyone around.

Hosea 8:7 (NKJV), "They sow the wind and reap the whirlwind."

Hosea 8:7 is my life verse. I know whatever I sow, that my sin does not affect me alone but everyone around me. Sin is the whirlwind that pushes into other's lives without their permission.

As the pain of sins was being exposed, and fearing the church might find out, isolation crept in. You see, take note, ladies, Satan loves to isolate us. We believe his lies when we are isolated. I felt alone. I became mad. Mad at God. Mad at the Church. I walked away. When I say I walked away, I walked away from the church and God. My dad was right about the church. I wanted no part of it. I started seeing all the ugly that church had within its walls.

The pain that walked around with me was heavy. It was my every thought, but I could not share my thoughts. I was not the one abused; however, that wind created a whirlwind and left a stockpile of damaged bodies/people lying around. The actual abuse and what we were going through was not discussed. We were not offered counseling. That closet was opened, and we pushed more skeletons in there. Everything that I knew was gone in a flash.

Life went on with our new normal. I quit going to church, and the further I was removed from the presence of people who walked with God, the easier it was to create my walk. This "new" me was so hurt and damaged that my motto became "I will hurt you before you hurt me". I had built walls around my heart and mind that allowed me to live as if nothing had happened. All the while, I began accumulating casualties within my cache of pain, inflicted upon others through my words, actions, and the course of my life.

I became a long-distance runner, literally and physically. When I got on the track, I would run those laps with only my thoughts, my breath, and my mental conversations. I took my pain back to where I first thought it happened. I am about fixing the hemorrhage, not putting a band-aid on it. I had child-like thinking and would practice while I ran what I would say to my grandfather, the man that represented "God" in my life - the man who took it all away.

The literal long-distance running was a learned trait to leave and go far away, so out of High School, I joined the military. It is the perfect place to learn how to disconnect from life and live out new dreams. I made my life something it was not by experiencing new worlds. I was a new person in the military. I had an instant family and I did things there that calmed my anger. The military gave me outlets. I also added sins to the tally list as I lived year by year, getting further away from God. I lived out this scripture:

Romans 1:28-32 (NKJV), "And even as they did not like to retain God in their knowledge, God gave them over to a debased mind, to do those things which are not fitting; being filled with all unrighteousness, sexual immorality, wickedness, covetousness, maliciousness; full of envy, murder, strife, deceit, evil-mindedness; they are whisperers, backbiters, haters of God, violent, proud, boasters, inventors of evil things, disobedient to parents, undiscerning, untrustworthy, unloving, unforgiving, unmerciful; who, knowing the righteous judgment of God, that those who practice such things are deserving of death, not only do the same but also approve of those who practice them.

Paul wrote this to me, so I will replace some words with my name so you can see. This is a practice that I do to show me how God's Word and scripture pertain to my life.

Romans 1:28-32 (NKJV)
And even as TAMMY did not like to retain God in HER knowledge, God gave HER over to a debased mind, to do those things which are not fitting; being filled with all unrighteousness, sexual immorality, wickedness, covetousness, maliciousness; full of envy, murder, strife, deceit, evil-mindedness; SHE IS A whisperer, backbiter, hater of God, violent, proud, boasters, inventors of evil things, disobedient to HER parent, undiscerning, untrustworthy, unloving, unforgiving, unmerciful; TAMMY knowing the righteous judgment of God, that those who practice such things are deserving of death, not only do the same but also approve of those who practice them.

RAISE UP

Ouch, it steps on my toes when I put my name in there. This was my life from my teens until my late twenties. I can now look back and call it what it is.....BUT GOD!

One night, after a series of bodies that I left behind due to choices that only gave me temporary feel-goods, a friend approached me. She was hurt and felt my actions had left her the same way I felt as a child. Everything we knew. GONE. We had a large friend group that we did life with. This group was fractured because I, once again chose my flesh in an attempt to be happy, to feel good, instead of thinking about what it would do to a friend. I took out my next victim. I was so self-absorbed. I never really felt what the other person experienced. I moved through life, ensuring I would never be hurt again. However, I continued to hurt every day.

Months prior, I had decided that I needed to change my life. I wrote out a life goals list and hung it up to read every day.

1) Find a man sent from God.
2) Finish RN School.
3) Change for my daughter.

I had my dad's Bible next to my bed on the nightstand. I held that Bible every night and cried myself to sleep for a year or more. I never opened it, as if it was like a child's security blanket that would give me comfort. I also can look back over the last many years and remember times when I would hear God's voice in my head. I would feel God's presence. I would sometimes say out loud, "Nope, I love you, God, but your way only provided pain". Childlike faith is equivalent to when you are swinging on a swing, falling off, and getting mad at the swing. I did not understand the fullness of the Gospel, and I had no one in my life share it with me.

Back to my friend. She told me she would pray for me that night, and she did not know who I was anymore.

Remember that kid that knew Jesus (yep me)? He was still in my heart and those words woke me out of a violent slumber. Those words, "I will pray for you." They sparked memories of who God was and that this life that I had manufactured, due to the sin of another, now had me in sin, living the same way, just not hidden in the closet. I lived this life in the wide open, not caring who saw and who was affected because I would not be a hypocrite. I would live Monday through Sunday the same way. I went home, and God kept me awake that night. I prayed. I asked God to help me.

A "Stalker" entered my life during the previous year. Insert rolling, crying, laughing emoji. This man was relentless and not taking no for an answer. We had become best friends. This stalker knew he would marry me. I said my life changed; however, it was not like a sonic boom, and immediately everything was back to following God only. I had to unlearn every vise and habit and thing I had survived over the past 13 years. I was messy. Over the course of a year, he showed up everywhere I was and we went on our first date. This date came with an agreement, one date, and he would never ask me again. I was so afraid of hurting him. I would tell people, and him, you are just too nice. Everything I ever prayed for in a partner, in a man, he embodied. He was kind, patient, and humble. He was fun and good-looking!

God heard the desires of my heart and answered. Why did God respond? Well, because he loves me. My desires lined up with His desires for me, for His Will. I prayed for a man sent from God. I found him in a bar - he came there because God sent him there to get me.

On our first date, he told me he wanted to marry and grow old with me; I hyperventilated. It was a push-away game, but he was always there, and I grew increasingly in love with him by the day. I remained in RN school. God was also helping me complete that prayer and life goal. The "Stalker" and I continued to date from the first date, and one night, I got him drunk to ask him a question.

Let me set up first why I asked this question: He had two children and I had one. I asked him, "Could we start taking the kids to church?" The look on his face. He asked why. I said, "I grew up in church, and I need to go back and heal, and I want the kids in church." We were around four months into dating. He agreed with the understanding that (HIS EXACT WORDS), "We will not be there every time those doors are open!" He also said we would not listen to Christian music and change our lives. I agreed. Four months into dating, we returned to the church, where the pain began for me as a child. I walked down that all-familiar aisle and past that third pew. I returned. Going back would provide the healing that I needed. My sister, Katie, was very instrumental in coming back. She was there to help me. When I passed that pew, my stomach leaped out of my mouth. I chose to sit on the second pew to the left side of it. I would look at that pew, and every childhood memory would come flooding back.

I knew God was taking me on a healing journey. You see, God never left me. I fled Him, but He remained in me through it all. No amount of alcohol or wildness could drown out the Holy Spirit's voice. I blamed Him for the pain but learned quickly the devil was to blame. I was hungry for the Word. The Pastor preached a sermon, and I hung on to every Word. We would attend Sunday School, and the deeper we got into God's Word, the more I needed. Our lives went through a radical change. There was this one thing; we were still living together in sin. I did not want to get married. I had the biggest fear of commitment. Marriage would be a forever thing. I had done that, and it did not work. Here we were at a spiritual crossroads.

We had been dating for six months and living together for about three months, and one day, I found a house for sale. I wanted it—the perfect Victorian home with the perfect picket fence. I told y'all that as a kid, I was a daydreamer. I need the ideal fairytale story. I called, and it had already gone under contract. I was devastated. Let's give the "stalker" a name, Wayne. In our kitchen, I was carrying on how that house was perfect, and I just wanted to have the ideal home to raise the perfect kids. He said, "Do you want to?" My response was, "Do I want to what?" "Do you want to make it official so we have the perfect family?"

My response was, "Well, I guess." Ladies, that was a fairy tale proposal. We laugh now; if he had got down on one knee and asked, I might have kicked him out of the house. We visited with the Pastor at the place that shaped my life, that little First Baptist Church. We went through pre-marital counseling and were told we were about to embark on the most challenging job any parent has, step-parenting. We announced to the family that we were getting married at a small wedding. Our next decision was one that we prayed over and decided that Wayne and I would be baptized together right after we married as our first act as husband and wife. We also committed to going to God first for everything before making decisions. We hurried to plan the wedding, wasting no time. I might run if it was an extended, drawn-out plan. I was changed; God had radically changed me. We did a cleansing that we had to do to focus on healing and our walk.

On our wedding day, I had rules—no music to march down to. My knees were knocking so loud and hard, Wayne, and I laughed. We were surrounded by some of our closest friends and our family. This man was an answer to my prayer; God picked him, I did not. The cool thing is God did know what He was doing. The baptism was my favorite part. We committed ourselves to Lord Jesus.

Remember Wayne saying he would not go to church every time the doors were open? Insert: on the ground rolling emoji. We were there every time the doors were open. It was the best. We raised our kids in that church. I would love to tell you the healing happened immediately, but it didn't. It was a slow process. I had many layers of pain; when one layer would be dealt with and peeled back, another layer of hurt was there. Hurt comes in many forms: Pain, anger, frustration, perfectionism, and works of the flesh; it is wild what the devil can put on you as ways to mask the pain or how you manifest it. My sweet husband was so gentle and kind during each new thing to heal from.

Now let us talk about my grandfather; I learned through my new journey with the Lord that there was much more to it than my childlike faith interpreted. God was not to blame. I needed to forgive. This one was the most challenging forgiveness that I have ever encountered. I kept thinking I had forgiven him, and then the devil would creep something in, or the light of God would show me an area I had not healed from. I never told my grandmother or my family that I knew everything. I was not supposed to know it all. Sometimes, as adults, you discuss things thinking kids are not listening. I heard it all that night (the night our lives changed), what he had done to each person, the damage he did. The closet door had started to creep open, and little by little, things seeped out. I made that man pay for what he did. I took on the role of teaching (do not miss the I in this - not what God would have, all me) him something about being a Christian, and the hate that came out of me was intense. Please do not miss the I in that statement. I had a lot of "I's" and forgot the "God instructs, God says."

My grandfather and I went to different churches by this point. The first time we encountered each other, he had open heart surgery and was hospitalized. My grandmother decided I would spend the night with him

RAISE UP

so he would not be alone when he woke up. She had no idea how I felt, what I knew. In my eyes, she was a saint, and I loved her so much. I could not tell her no. I stayed. The look on his face when he woke up, and I was sitting there. I was sitting in that chair with my Bible in my lap, reading it because I had rehearsed what I would say to him my whole life. I just smiled and said "you got me". I became his caregiver that night, and he knew how hurt I was. He questioned why I agreed to stay with him. I explained that I loved my grandmother, and so he got me. Even now, these are hard words to write. I did not want to be there, but it is what it is. I was ugly but had compassion for him. At that moment, I felt sorry for him. I would never have left my dad in the hospital, but I was the only one there for him. He did ask for my forgiveness, and I did accept it. In a very sarcastic way, I received it and let him know, "only because God told me I had to, but it would not change our relationship."

Over the years, we had many encounters, and more healing would happen each time. My grandmother was sick and needed a nurse, so I was her nurse. When I came in, my grandfather would visit with me and then leave us to do our thing. Our thing was eating peppermint Lamar's candies and listening to the Gaithers on record. I loved her; I loved her walk with the Lord.

Back to my raise-up story. We raised our kids in church and I entered Church Ministry as a vocation. I have never looked back. Every promise in scripture is for me. God forgave me for every sin to every person and myself that I did. My life was different. I had a perfect marriage, and I mean perfect. He is everything that God talks about in a helper and husband. Remember the statement that being a step-parent was the hardest thing you would do; actually, it has been relatively easy. When you commit to raising your kids sold out for Jesus, or at least every decision you make, you take it to the Lord first; it is easier when life throws things your way. Our kids are typical, now adult kids. They had everyday worldly things pop up, but we got through them and always gave God the credit where it was due.

Many years back, our grandson passed away. He was born early and was with us for a short while. We had my grandson's funeral, and there was enough seating for the immediate family. Since I was the step-parent, I took my place in the back, standing up. I love the back of the room; it is like an armor-bearer station, a great place to pray. As I was back there, I glanced over to my left, and my grandfather stood there. He had come. He came quietly. He was present. I thought back a few months ago, and God showed me that he came, my most challenging day, and my grandfather was there for me. He did not personally know my two St. (they are saints, not step) Kids, but his love for me was present that day. A few months later, my grandfather went into a coma. I was asked to sit by his bedside, and then I had him moved home so he could pass away at home. I learned afterward that he had confessed every sin he ever did and asked for forgiveness. My grandfather wanted me to know. I believed that my walk with God showed him a new way. His Pastor told me how proud he was of me and that when he left this world, he went in right standing with God. Salvation and forgiveness are for everyone; you must accept them and walk by His Word. I will see him again in the cloud of witnesses when I enter heaven's gates.

    I thank God for His voice and for constantly chasing and speaking to me. I live my life to share the love of Jesus with everyone. I want women to know their true identity in Christ and the freedom Christ offers if you live committed to Jesus Christ as your Lord and Savior. I chose a committed life to Christ; it is not boring but fun! I decided that the generational sins would not affect my family. I try to live ALIVE, Abundantly Living In Victory Eternally (right now, tomorrow, and every day after).

Romans 8: 5-6 (NKJV), "For those who live according to the flesh set their minds on the things of the flesh, but those who live according to the Spirit, the things of the Spirit. For to be carnally minded is death, but to be spiritually minded is life and peace."

    I had to change from a worldly mindset to a spiritual mindset. You must first know the character of God. The Holy Spirit is with me as a gift of salvation. I chose to have Him at the center of my life, which activated that to be a part of my being, and then I became fully alive. Sometimes, I forget this, which is evident, so getting in God's Word, the Holy Bible, keeps me grounded. I chose to live alive by forgiving, throwing off bitterness and anger, and crawling out of the casket I had created for myself, and the devil helped me put the nails in the coffin. I chose to forgive quickly and pray for the person. People are messy. I am messy.

RAISE UP

Each day, I pray that I meet one person for Jesus, and by my presence, they find hope in Christ. They see what I have and want more for their lives; they want this walk.

As I write this, we will celebrate 24 years of marriage and we now have four kids. Our children are raised as siblings, not stepkids or blended families. I am blessed with what we call a spiritual daughter, this is one that I have no legal rights to, but God gave her to me, and I get to serve in ministry with her. We have eight grandkids and more to come. I have committed to saying yes to God when it comes to ministry; if He says go, then we go. I have faithfully served local church ministry for 25 years and nationally since 2019. I now travel to share what God lays on my heart with women nationwide.

Closing thought: You can live a life serving yourself and running because of the pain that another caused you, but it only leads to more pain. God is your ultimate healer, your comforter, and will make everything work together for good. Let your comeback story define who you are in Christ, living in freedom and not in bondage to the one who caused you the pain.

Never tell God what you are not going to do! We are at the church every time the doors open and even go into churches we don't attend. You are worthy of a life covered in joy, hope, and love. Jesus gives that all! Last, someone is depending on you to share the Gospel of Jesus Christ with them. They need you!

Reflect and Write Your Story
Addressing Generational Sin

Reflect:

In what way does the personal story you've just read connect with your own experiences? Is there common ground between you and the author? Explore the emotions you felt while reading. Where do those feelings stem from and how are they connected to your personal story?

RAISE UP

Writing Prompt:
Analyze patterns or cycles that have emerged in your personal or family history. Explore how these recurrent themes have influenced your journey. Describe a specific instance where you successfully broke a detrimental cycle. Detail the steps you took, the challenges you encountered, and the transformative effects of your actions on shaping a new direction.

Scripture Connection:
Can you see where God was in this part of your story? Do any scriptures come to mind?

Chapter Nine
Jessica Cornelison

JESSICA CORNELISON

Jessica's Blessing:
Adoption's Path To Multiplying Faith

Have you ever had a time in your life where you were just moving along and in a moment it seemed like everything was tipped on its head? It could have been for good or for bad, but suddenly everything changed. Maybe it was something you thought to be true and you suddenly found out it wasn't. Maybe you thought you really knew someone and then you found out something that completely changed your idea of who that person was. Maybe you felt like you were stuck in a position or a relationship and suddenly there was a way out. Whatever the case may be, we have all had a moment, some of us more than one, where everything changed.

In that moment, what do you do? If it's a good change, you probably rejoice, maybe thank the Lord and go tell everyone about the good news. But, what if it's a hard change? What if you just lost your job or a relationship, received a bad diagnosis from the doctor or found out something that you just can't comprehend? Whether this change is mainly physical, emotional or spiritual, what do you do? Do you look at the information objectively to see if you need to change something? Do you ignore the new information that has been presented because it doesn't fit what you believe and you don't want to have to deal with it? Do you shut everyone out and just shut down because you don't know what to do? Or do you go to scripture for guidance in the midst of the turmoil? Do you go to God in prayer and seek His will in the situation? Do you call on your brothers and sisters in Christ and ask them to join you in prayer?

Philippians 4:6-7 (NIV) says, *"Do not be anxious about anything, but in every situation, by prayer and petition, with thanksgiving, present your requests to God. And the peace of God, which transcends all understanding, will guard your hearts and your minds in Christ Jesus."* In James 1:5 (NIV) we read, *"If any of you lacks wisdom, you should ask God, who gives generously to all without finding fault, and it will be given to you."* In 1 Thessalonians 5:17 (NLT), we simply find the words, *"Never stop praying."* If scripture, which is the written word of God, says that we are supposed to go to Him in everything, why do we so often leave that as a last resort?

    Scripture tells us time and time again that God never changes and that He hears our prayers. So, why wouldn't we want to rely on a God that never changes instead of relying on our own strength which has failed us time and time again? Why wouldn't we want to rely on a God who grants peace beyond understanding, instead of relying on our own wisdom, when our thoughts and desires can change from day to day? Scripture is full of these promises from the Lord telling us that we don't have to figure out the direction. All we need to do, is hand the situation over to Him and take the steps He gives us, as seen in Proverbs 3:5-6 (NIV), *"Trust in the Lord with all your heart and lean not on your own understanding; in all your ways submit to him, and he will make your paths straight."* That seems like a pretty clear direction, but how often do we rely on our own strength and understanding, even when our personal beliefs and convictions have been flipped upside down and we can't seem to see straight? I wish I could say that I have this down and going to God in prayer is always my first response, but that response is still being cultivated in me.

    I want to take a moment to tell you the story of a young girl. This girl grew up in a loving, Christian home. She always knew she was adopted and she knew her parents loved her more than anything. When she was three, her parents accepted two foster children, ages three and six. She was so excited to meet these new girls and the first thing she said when they arrived was, "This is my mom and dad, now let's go play." She promptly took them to her room and showed them all the toys. All that mattered in that moment was that they knew who her parents were and that she was ready to play. About a year later, the girls were officially adopted and could also say "This is my mom and dad."

    Now, as I said, this was very much a Christian home. They were always in church if the doors were open and her parents even taught

JESSICA CORNELISON

Sunday School classes. When she was five, her parents were called into the ministry. The family sold their home and moved to a town about 4 hours away so the dad could go to Seminary and become a pastor. Upon finishing seminary, the family spent the summer at Inks Lake State Park in Burnet, where the dad was the Park Chaplain for the summer. They had so much fun! The girls attended just about every VBS in the area, helped put on skits for the kids visiting the park, helped host fishing competitions and they even had church services and movie nights in the outdoor amphitheater. It was a great summer!

After that summer, the dad began pastoring a church just down the road from where they lived. It was a small church by the name of Victory Baptist and at the age of 7, the girl accepted the Lord as her savior and was baptized. Now, being a small church in a country town, they didn't have a baptismal, but they did have a hot tub that someone donated to the church. You read that right, that little girl was baptized in her backyard, by her father, in a hot tub, with the whole church family there to support her. I mean how many people get to say that they were baptized by their own father, but to be baptized in a hot tub seemed like the coolest thing!

The next few years brought a lot of changes. The family adopted a little boy, the mom started homeschooling the girls and then the family made a move to Kentucky where the dad pastored another small Baptist church. While their stay in Kentucky was short, the girls had great fun participating in puppet ministry and were even able to attend puppet competitions! After 2 years in Kentucky, it was time to leave the church, but the family didn't know where they were going. To allow them some time to plan, the parents decided to just put a sign in the yard marking the house for sale rather than listing it through a realtor. Believe it or not, that house sold in five days! Not knowing where to go yet, the family loaded almost all of their belongings into a semi-trailer, parked it at a friend's house and moved into a 30' RV in which they ended up traveling around the country for almost 9 months. Now, 9 months in a 30' RV with six people and a dog will either make or break you as a family.

As I mentioned earlier, this girl and her siblings were homeschooled. While the majority of their travels took place over the summer and they did some schooling on the road, after 9 months, they really needed to find a place to settle down and get the rest of their school books out of storage. The family spent a lot of time in prayer and reaching out to different churches, trying to figure out where they were supposed to go. They came very close to moving to Bolivia, which is a story for another day, but after lots of prayer, the family ended up in Marble Falls, Texas. As God would have it, they even ended up purchasing land and building their home just a half mile down the road from the house that little girl first called home!

    Now, as you've probably guessed at this point, that little girl is me. For the longest time growing up, I felt like I didn't really have a good testimony. I mean, I grew up in a Christian home, I had parents that loved me, I never drank or did drugs or broke the law, so what kind of story was there for me to tell other people? It took me a long time to truly see that my story wasn't some big turn-around, but rather a story of God's never-ending faithfulness to me. That doesn't mean that there haven't been many hard times in my life, but throughout each situation, I can clearly look back and see God's steady hand. Let's take a quick look back at some of those situations.

    Remember that baby boy that we adopted when I was 7 years old? Imagine all of that joy of having a baby brother and loving him for five months only to be told that the birth mother changed her mind and wanted him back. Sounds crazy, right? But that's what happened to us. Five months of loving this boy, taking care of him, having him as a part of our family and one day we are told we have to give him back. We knew the home situation he was coming from wasn't a very good one, so we decided to fight back. So followed two years of court dates and visitations. Every other Friday we would be picked up early from school, drive the 4 hours to Austin to pick him up, drive 4 hours back home, have our time with my brother and then Sunday after church we would make the trip again to drop him back off. Taking him back was always so hard and never got any easier. He would be upset and not want to leave us and we would spend the whole trip home just crying. There were many times we had to pull off the side of the road because we were all just grieving and even mom and dad couldn't hold it together for the four-hour drive home until they'd had a good cry.

    So, where was God's hand of faithfulness in taking that little boy away? Isaiah 65:24 in the New Living Translation says, *"I will answer them before they even call to me. While they are still talking about their needs, I will go ahead and answer their prayers!"* Let me show you what God saw that we would only see after the fact. God saw that lives would be saved in the midst of this trial. The process started with his entire biological family and about five lawyers against us and our one lawyer. Over the course of those two years, some of his family started to see that we truly wanted what was best for him and started to believe that we were it. Close to the end of those two years, many of his family were on our side and some of them even started sneaking us extra visitation days. Some of those family members saw something different in us and had us walk them through accepting the Lord as their savior while we were still fighting in court! Because of that process, when we moved back to the area years later and started a church, many of those family members that wouldn't attend a regular church started coming to our church and even more of them were saved!

We never would have made it through those two years if we didn't surround ourselves in prayer and have a community that covered us in prayer and support. *"Call to me and I will answer you and tell you great and unsearchable things you do not know."* (Jeremiah 33:3, NIV) We spent a lot of time crying out to the Lord and asking why this was happening and what we were supposed to do. He simply said to be patient and told us that we would get him back. Although two years seems like a very long time, in God's eyes, is two years not worth it to bring so many of His children back to Him? Not only were some of the family members saved, many of whom we still talk to today, but the story was also a testimony of God's love to those around us.

Let's take a look at another part of the story. Remember how my family traveled around the country for 9 months? Well, I was 13 at that time and one day during the trip, my mom asked me a question. She said, "If you know something important, but you know it will hurt someone to tell them, should you tell them anyways." Being a typical 13 year old, I didn't really have a solid response to that, but mom said she thought that the answer was "yes" and proceeded to tell me a story. It was a story about my birth, but it was different than the story I already knew and, as a 13 year old, it completely changed my world.

RAISE UP

Do you remember how that little girl always knew she was adopted? Not only did I know I was adopted, I would also talk to my biological mom on the phone sometimes and decided to meet her for the first time when I was five. We met at a restaurant in town and I met my biological brother and sister for the first time as well. That's right, I have an older brother and a younger sister from my biological mom. Over the years I've tried to maintain a relationship with them and while sometimes were harder than others to stay in touch, I always try to keep in contact.

Now, as far as I had always known, my birth mom couldn't afford to take care of me when I was born and so she made the decision to give me up for adoption so I could have a better life. I knew that she already had a two year old boy at the time she was pregnant with me and that she had trouble taking care of him, so giving me up was the best choice. While this was mostly true, during this conversation I found out that there was more to this decision than I had originally known.

While my birth mom did decide to give me up for adoption, that wasn't actually her first choice. When she realized she wouldn't be able to care for a second child, her plan was to get an abortion. She didn't just think about getting an abortion, but she had the doctor's visit planned! After some changes in her doctor's schedule and some conversations with the lady that was currently helping to care for her 2 year old son, she agreed to consider adoption. Once adoption was decided upon, the adoptive family, my parents, went with her to all of her doctor's appointments and were even at the hospital when I was born.

Now, yes, this sounds like a happy ending, but imagine being 13 years old and being told that your biological mom wanted to have an abortion. Hearing this information at 13 was devastating emotionally. It was like my entire world was flipped upside down. Suddenly, I went from knowing I was given up because that was the best choice for me, to feeling like I was unwanted and my birth mom just wanted to get rid of me. I began to question everything I knew about myself. I knew I had an older brother and a younger sister, so I started to question "Why me? Why was I the one she didn't want? Why wasn't I good enough?"

Yes, I spent a lot of time praying after receiving this news, however, I wasn't truly seeking and listening for the Lord's response. It was more of a time spent sharing my heartache and crying out to the Lord in pain. I spent many nights crying and praying and asking why this knowledge was even shared with me. I went from being confident in who I was to questioning everything. I was suddenly afraid of failing, afraid of being rejected by others, afraid I wasn't good enough and afraid I would let people down and they would leave me. I was afraid to go to places or events that I wasn't specifically invited to, and even some that I was, because "what if people didn't actually want me there". I was suddenly afraid that I just wasn't enough.

    Throughout this time, I did ask the Lord to soften my heart towards my birth mom. As I said, I had known her growing up and she would come visit us from time to time with my brother and sister. After this revelation though, I wasn't quite sure how I was going to face her. It did take a while, but shortly after we settled back in Marble Falls, I was ready to meet her again. We got together and I told her that I knew the whole story. I was able to tell her that I forgave her for wanting to make that choice and that I was so appreciative she made the decision to adopt in the end. While I was able to forgive her in that moment, it didn't mean that the pain went away.

    Let's fast forward to college. I've forgiven my birth mom, we still get together from time to time, but at heart, I'm still a young girl questioning everything. I didn't attend events unless my roommates specifically invited me and sometimes it took some convincing on their part to get me to agree. It was almost like, if they weren't willing to fight to get me to come, then they must not really want me there. I know as you read those words, it can sound crazy, but for someone that has a fear of being unwanted or being left alone, one of your worst fears is being at an event, surrounded by people, and feeling like no one would care if you were there or not. Unfortunately, in my case, that also came hand-in-hand with a fear of being left out. So, if they didn't convince me to come, then I would stay in the room, by myself, and question why they didn't want me to be a part of whatever they were doing.

    Throughout this time I continued to try and maintain a relationship with my birth mom and siblings. I would call to check in and try and arrange times to get together, but I would always end the calls feeling like I was the only one putting in the effort to keep the relationship. I remember one day calling to just check-in. I asked what they were up to and the response was, "Oh, we're on our way to your brother's wedding." I quickly said, "Oh, okay, have fun and give him a hug for me,"

RAISE UP

and I hung up the phone. I promptly broke down crying because I didn't even know that he had a girlfriend, let alone that he was getting married. In my mind, this just reinforced the idea that they didn't want a relationship with me. Once again, I was unwanted.

I remember one of my friends coming outside, sitting next to me on the porch of our campus apartment, putting his arm around my shoulder and just holding me as I cried. No questions asked. I felt like I was inconveniencing him, so I started to apologize and tried to get up and go be by myself. He just pulled me back down, said I didn't have to apologize for being upset and continued to sit there until I was done crying. At that moment, I was convinced that I was done trying to have a relationship with people that didn't care about me.

Now I know you're asking yourself, okay, where was God's hand in this situation? Where can we see God's hand in the midst of this heartache and sorrow? It's there, subtly woven between the lines of the story. Remember those changes in the doctor's schedule? Those changes were actually family emergencies that caused the doctor to cancel the scheduled appointment. That cancellation led the birth mom to revisit a conversation about the possibility of adopting which she had previously turned down. You can't tell me that God's fingerprints aren't all over that!

Let's also take a look at the situation of the adoptive parents. They had just been married 3 months when a friend of theirs asked if they would be interested in adopting. When they met the birth mom for the first time, it turned out they already knew each other! You see, months and months earlier the adoptive mom was cleaning at a business. The owner mentioned that her daughter needed someone to help watch her son and so she recommended a friend of hers. If you haven't already guessed it, that daughter ended up being my biological mom and that friend was the one that connected them back together to arrange for an adoption.

Jeremiah 1:5a (NIV) says, *"Before I formed you in the womb I knew you, before you were born I set you apart;"* and Jeremiah 29:11 (NIV) says, *"For I know the plans I have for you,"* declares the Lord, *"plans to prosper you and not to harm you, plans to give you hope and a future."* God set His plans into motion before I was even a thought in my birth mom's mind. While she was planning for an abortion, He was making plans of His own. Even though my siblings and I come from three different families (DNA-wise), God put us together forming one new family. He interceded in each of our lives, placing us together.

While I can look back now and point to where His hand was in these situations, it wasn't an easy thing for me to see at first. Thankfully, I had a wonderful group of individuals surrounding me when I was at college. One of the biggest steps in starting to change my perspective again was a conversation during a chapel service in college. At the end of the service, I ended up talking with our BSM (Baptist Student Ministries) Director. It was the next service after that phone conversation where I broke down crying. I was pouring out my heart to her and just shared everything about the situation. She hugged me, prayed with me and then offered a new perspective of the story to cling to.

You see, instead of looking at the opening of the story and focusing on being unwanted, we looked at the end of the story. In the end, my parents didn't have to adopt me, but they chose to. They chose to attend those doctor's appointments, be at the hospital and take me home as their daughter. In reality, I was wanted! That was the beginning, the awakening, of recognizing my true identity in Christ. Instead of being unwanted, I was chosen, set apart, and most importantly, I was the daughter of the King!

Now, gaining this new perspective didn't mean that all the hurt and feelings went away overnight. To be honest, I still struggle with those feelings from time to time. They are the enemy's greatest weapon against me. But, because I recognize that, I can fight against them. I can speak truth into the lies that I'm not enough, that I'm unwanted, that I'm a disappointment or that I'm going to fail. I can speak truth because I surround myself with those that can speak truth over me.

Once I flipped the script back over in my mind, I started to slowly venture outside of my comfort zone. During Spiritual Emphasis Week at college, a missionary came to speak in one of my classes. I went up and talked to him afterwards, something I never would have done before, and Stephen and I became friends. I started attending prayer meetings at his house and it was by far the most amazing thing I had ever been a part of. These prayer meetings were where the Lord truly began to cultivate my heart. We would worship, people would pray or start playing or singing songs as they felt led, people would speak out words from the Lord as they received them, without fear, and it was such a beautiful time with the Lord. During these meetings, I began to journal. I found that through journaling, I really channeled my communication with the Lord. Sometimes I would write prayers to Him and sometimes I would just start writing without really knowing what I was writing. When I would go back and read them, they would be answers from Him!

During this time of cultivation, I grew so much closer to the Lord. In many of my writings there are phrases such as, "Where you call me Lord, I will go" and "Send me where you want me." Little did I know that I was being prepared to truly go. I attended these prayer meetings for my last year and a half at college and even afterwards, sometimes I would drive the hour and a half back to Belton to attend them. My parents even drove up to attend a few meetings because they wanted to check out what was going on and they ended up becoming friends with Stephen and his wife. Over the years, they remained friends of our family, and my sister even lived in his mom's house for a while when she started working in that town after graduation. To this day, the Lord could tell him to get on a plane and he will get on it, not knowing anyone on the other side, and yet, there is always someone there to meet him that the Lord has sent! Oh, that we would be so willing to just go when He tells us to go!

Now, I mentioned being prepared to go and I'm sure you're wondering, "Go where?" Well, over the course of three years, I had three different people tell me that I was going to end up in Africa. Yes, Africa! One person said they could see me surrounded by children in African garb while another said that I would be approached about going and I wouldn't have to seek it out. I continued to tell the Lord that I would go if He wanted, but it didn't happen immediately. I worked as an Activities Supervisor for two years and an Activities Manager for a little over a year at a resort down the road from us. During this time, I still had those words in my mind about going to Africa someday.

Well, wouldn't you know it, in 2014 I quit my job, not knowing what I was going to do next, just knowing I wasn't supposed to be in that job anymore. After a few months of praying and trying to find a new job, an opportunity arose to teach at a school in Africa. Now, when I say someone told me that I would be approached about going and I wouldn't have to seek it out, not even I could have predicted the true meaning of being approached.

I received a phone call one day from my dad, stating that missionaries from Africa had come to the house so their kids could go horseback riding. They needed a third grade teacher and wanted to know if they could meet with me right then. To say I was stunned, would be an understatement. I ended up meeting with their daughter the next day and four weeks later, I was in Africa! Talk about being pushed out of your comfort zone. I went from not going anywhere I wasn't invited, to flying halfway around the world by myself to a country where I knew no one. I signed up to teach for one year and ended up staying for five!

Upon leaving Malawi, I went to China to teach. I had planned to be there for two years, but God had other plans. Covid broke out halfway through my first year, so I came back home and finished teaching the year online. Clearly, the Lord was protecting me in that also as the school I was at was only about a 2 1/2 hour drive from Wuhan, where the virus broke out. As soon as flights started to get canceled, I booked a flight and I was able to get out right away.

Through every circumstance or trial, from fighting for my brother, to struggling with feeling unwanted, to amazing prayer meetings, to quitting my job and moving to Malawi and then China, the Lord has always had His hand in my life. At times, it can be a little hard to see, but I've learned to just sit back, watch and take life one step at a time. If I feel like I'm not receiving an answer from the Lord on something, then maybe what He is really saying is that I need to be quiet and wait, because I'm right where He wants me to be for the moment.

So, when you have those moments in your life where everything changes, what are you going to do? Are you going to rely on your own strength and wisdom? Or will you go to God in prayer and seek His will in the situation? Will you go to the scriptures for guidance in the midst of turmoil? Will you call on your brothers and sisters in Christ to cover you in prayer and support? Remember that God is the only one that has always been and will always be, the only one who sees the past, present and future. He's given us a glimpse of the end of the story, so don't you think we can rely on Him to get us through any trial we may face?

RAISE UP

I love the way The Message writes Matthew 6:25-34:

"If you decide for God, living a life of God-worship, it follows that you don't fuss about what's on the table at mealtimes or whether the clothes in your closet are in fashion. There is far more to your life than the food you put in your stomach, more to your outer appearance than the clothes you hang on your body. Look at the birds, free and unfettered, not tied down to a job description, careless in the care of God. And you count far more to him than birds.

Has anyone by fussing in front of the mirror ever gotten taller by so much as an inch? All this time and money wasted on fashion - do you think it makes that much difference? Instead of looking at the fashions, walk out into the fields and look at the wildflowers. They never primp or shop, but have you ever seen color and design quite like it? The ten best-dressed men and women in the country look shabby alongside them.

If God gives such attention to the appearance of wildflowers - most of which are never even seen - don't you think he'll attend to you, take pride in you, do his best for you? What I'm trying to do here is to get you to relax, to not be so preoccupied with getting, so you can respond to God's giving. People who don't know God and the way he works fuss over these things, but you know both God and how he works. Steep your life in God-reality, God-initiative, God-provisions. Don't worry about missing out. You'll find all your everyday human concerns will be met.

Give your entire attention to what God is doing right now, and don't get worked up about what may or may not happen tomorrow. God will help you deal with whatever hard things comes up when the time comes."

JESSICA CORNELISON

Reflect and Write Your Story
Adoption's Path To Multiplying Faith

Reflect:

In what way does the personal story you've just read connect with your own experiences? Is there common ground between you and the author? Explore the emotions you felt while reading. Where do those feelings stem from and how are they connected to your personal story?

RAISE UP

Writing Prompt:

Reflect and describe the catalyst that prompted you to seek healing, exploring the emotions and thoughts that accompanied this decision. Delve into any scriptures that provided peace or guidance during this process. Share how these scriptures resonated with you and contributed to your healing journey.

JESSICA CORNELISON

Scripture Connection:

Looking back, can you see where God was in this part of your story? Do any scriptures come to mind?

Chapter Ten
Victoria Steelman

VICTORIA STEELMAN

Victoria's Transformation:
A Journey From Single To Blended Family

Since I can remember, I have always loved the movie "It's a wonderful life." I love to watch George's journey and that dynamic ending! That moment he finally gets it after he glances what the world would have been like had he never been born. We have all had those moments where we wonder if our time here has genuinely mattered. To know me is to know that I want my life to count for something wonderful for my Lord and Savior, Jesus Christ, and that I try to live out the scripture with all my heart.

John 13:35 KJV *"By this shall all men know that ye are my disciples if ye have love for one another."*

I have heard it said there are five gospels: Matthew, Mark, Luke, John, and me, and we may be the only gospel some people will ever read. What will be their interpretation of who Jesus is in reading us? Will we represent our Lord well, or fail as one of His ambassadors, leaving them with a bad taste in their mouths and causing them to lose faith in Him? As believers in Christ, your life and how you live it truly matters. None of us are perfect, but we, as followers of Christ, should be moving closer to our Lord and Savior. When we do, we will grow in Him and His ways, looking, acting, and behaving increasingly like Him, becoming stronger and stronger in our walks and, in turn, naturally becoming a better representation of Him for others to see.

1 Peter 1:14-16 (NIV), "As obedient children, do not conform to the evil desires you had when you lived in ignorance. But just as he who called you is holy, so be holy in all you do; for it is written: "Be holy because I am holy."

RAISE UP

Galatians 5:16-24 (NIV), "So I say, walk by the Spirit, and you will not gratify the desires of the flesh. For the flesh desires what is contrary to the Spirit, and the Spirit what is contrary to the flesh. They are in conflict with each other, so that you are not to do whatever you want. But if you are led by the Spirit, you are not under the law. The acts of the flesh are obvious: sexual immorality, impurity and debauchery; idolatry and witchcraft; hatred, discord, jealousy, fits of rage, selfish ambition, dissensions, factions and envy; drunkenness, orgies, and the like. I warn you, as I did before, that those who live like this will not inherit the kingdom of God. But the fruit of the Spirit is love, joy, peace, forbearance, kindness, goodness, faithfulness, gentleness and self-control. Against such things there is no law. Those who belong to Christ Jesus have crucified the flesh with its passions and desires."

As you read my story, I pray you are encouraged to know that if God can use me, He can use you too! The Lord uses strange or foolish things to confound the wise.

"But God chose what is foolish in the world to shame the wise; God chose what is weak in the world to shame the strong; God chose what is low and despised in the world, even things that are not, to bring to nothing things that are, so that no human being might boast in the presence of God. And because of him, you are in Christ Jesus, who became to us wisdom from God, righteousness and sanctification and redemption, so that, as it is written, "Let the one who boasts, boast in the Lord." (1 Corinthians 1:27-31, ESV)

I often say I am a "strange thing" because the Lord has called me to sit at tables that, by worldly standards, I have no business being. He uses me to minister on platforms that only He has made possible. The Lord is truly faithful, and He will ALWAYS get the glory for all the good things in my life. Any talents I have come from Him and are fueled through His anointing.

Ok, hold on tight; here we go! I was born in Nashville, Tennessee. My parents are Joe and Ann Rhoden. My father was a country music singer who moved my mother to Nashville before I was born to try to make it big in Country Music. Tragically, that was not to be. He was electrocuted while welding at his day job and died at 32 years old, leaving my mother living in a trailer park in Nashville with three small children and pregnant with my little sister. I was a year and a half old at the time of my father's death. The night before my father died, my mother told me he was lying on the floor with me, bouncing on his back while trying to sing, "He's got the whole world in His hands." He told my mother I would be their little singer, and he was right.

I have always sung, and because of the call on my life, I am best when I minister for Him or sing for Him! I have had a call on my life since I can remember to be used by the Lord to travel the world and encourage others through my music and ministry.

It is funny how the enemy works. When you give your life to The Lord, you instantly become a threat to him. The enemy will then try to discourage and extinguish the threat. He will use people in the world to hurt you and those closest to you. Since I gave my heart to Jesus at seven years old, I have faced countless battles, and as my friend Thresa says, "I walk with a limp", spiritually but not physically. I am thankful for that limp because with it comes the knowledge that I can do all things through Christ who strengthens me! I have been wounded deeply in the battles, but have overcome them because of The Holy Spirit within me; He has raised me up out of the pits I have put myself in more times than I like to recollect. The Lord has proven His love and faithfulness to me time and time again.

Psalm 40:2-4 (KJV), "He brought me up also out of a horrible pit, out of the miry clay, and set my feet upon a rock, and established my goings. And he hath put a new song in my mouth, even praise unto our God: many shall see it, and fear, and shall trust in the Lord. Blessed is that man that maketh the Lord his trust, and respecteth not the proud, nor such as turn aside to lies."

I, however, have not always been as faithful to him. With regret, I can say I have not responded correctly to every situation I have faced. I have failed God more times than I care to mention, and it is only by His grace that I am here today, whole in Him, living in Victory!

RAISE UP

One of my favorite passages is:

1 Peter 5:8-11 (NIV), "Be alert and of sober mind. Your enemy, the devil prowls around like a roaring lion looking for someone to devour. Resist him, standing firm in the faith, because you know that the family of believers throughout the world is undergoing the same kind of sufferings. And the God of all grace, who called you to his eternal glory in Christ, after you have suffered a little while, will himself restore you and make you strong, firm and steadfast. To him be the power forever and ever. Amen."

Had I learned to be more alert earlier, I could have known how to fight the enemy and overcome his schemes. Had I stayed close to The Lord in high school and learned just how much Jesus loves me, I would not have felt unloved, hopeless, and wanting to take my own life. I will never forget the night I was laying in my bed, overcome with sadness, allowing the enemy to bombard my mind with painless ways to end my life when the Lord spoke to me, "If you hold on, your life will be better than you ever dreamed" I knew nothing about taking my thoughts captive, but when He spoke that to me, it gave me hope that I would make it through my current situation.

2 Corinthians 10:5-6 (KJV), "Casting down imaginations, and every high thing that exalteth itself against the knowledge of God, and bringing into captivity every thought to the obedience of Christ; and having in a readiness to revenge all disobedience, when your obedience is fulfilled."

Desperate to make "Better than I ever dreamed" happen, I started looking for love in all the wrong places, looking for that knight in shining armor to come to save me. If I had been patient, I would not have run away from home with an older man only to find myself pregnant. Had I not been so naïve, I would have understood I was pregnant with a baby, not just a fetus. I would not have made the horrible choice to have an abortion to cover up my sin and not shame my family any more than I had already.

Firstly, I was too young to make a decision of that magnitude. One that would not only take the life of my unborn child but would leave me crippled in shame, feeling forever bound in believing the lies of the enemy that I was dirty and unusable by God. I carried that shame, believing those lies for most of my life. I would try to follow the call to minister and sing to encourage others, but I would always stop because of the lies I believed.

So, I learned how to minister where I was as best as possible and tried to be happy. I would minister behind the chair as a cosmetologist, behind the camera as a photographer, behind the walls of my church in the choir, and through teaching Sunday school for the youth. I was bursting at the seams to fulfill my call without drawing too much attention to myself. I had grown at peace with it and learned to face the fact that this would be the closest I would get to ministering to The World. I ministered with all the passion I could, because I knew I had messed it up and could never fully live out my call.

The Lord led me to start a Facebook blog/vlog ministry called "Tuesday's Encouraging Word," Jesus in 5 Minutes or Less, which I posted on my ministry page weekly. I felt safe because I filmed it myself behind the safety of my phone and social media. Each week for over two years, I ministered through it. I did not know that The Lord would minister to me and raise me up to finally live in freedom through it.

My friend, Sheri Snow, called me and asked me to help her friend, Julie - who was coming into Nashville from out of town - with her hair for a benefit she was going to. I had never met her, but I had never met a stranger, so I arranged to meet her and style her hair.

I will never forget that day. It was during the court proceedings Judge Brett M. Kavanaugh was facing and I was interceding that day for him. I knew I had to fight spiritually for him because adding him to the supreme court would help overturn Roe v. Wade. While I could not undo what I had done over 31 years ago, I could help fight for the lives of future babies. I got to her hotel room and asked if I could turn on the TV to stay focused and pray for him.

Not wanting to be rude, Julie and I conversed briefly while I was there. She asked me about myself, and I told her about my fledgling ministry. She asked me if I would come on her show, Julie and Friends on TCT network to talk about my ministry. I had never seen her show, and I felt a little embarrassed because I did not have much of a ministry, but the Lord spoke to me and told me to say yes, so I did. I had no idea that Julie Noland was the daughter of Garth W. and Tina Coonce, the owners of TCT Network. I am glad I didn't know! I would have struggled with my decision if I had known. It was one of those strange things I felt unqualified for, but I wanted to obey The Lord. I had spent my whole life with a call on my life to minister and sing, but because of the guilt and shame of the abortion, I would struggle to live out my calling fully. I had cut short the life of my unborn child, so who was I to live out mine?

My actions as a young girl kept me debilitated for most of my adult life, but I proceeded forward. I thought I was prepared for the interview when the Lord spoke to me three weeks before we were to tape it and said, "it's time to talk about your abortion". That stopped me in my tracks. I spent the next three weeks curled up in a ball on the couch. I would cry and argue with God. I had held onto that horrible secret for 31 years. I would cry out to God, "but everyone would know", and I could not face that. I just knew my children, friends, and family would all hate me. Would I be burned at the stake? Would they hate me forever? I could not do it! The Lord would not budge, so I had to face the fact that 31 years after that dreadful day, God would make me share my horrible secret and not only that, but on worldwide television.

My husband, Barry, and I were driving up for me to be on the show, and I knew I had to call Julie and tell her. Julie answered the phone and listened to me as I was crying. I began telling her what God had told me to share. To my shock, Julie responded differently than I had anticipated. She responded in love and was so gracious to me. She said that in all her years of hosting the show, no one had ever shared their story of abortion. Julie ministered to me that she believed that my story would minister to so many and that it would save lives as well. That gave my heart hope, and the overwhelming fear of what people thought about me began to fade away. I began to feel optimistic that the death of my child could be redeemed in some small way through my story being shared in front of millions. At that moment, Romans 8:28 (AMP) poured over me. *"And we know [with great confidence] that God [who is deeply concerned about us] causes all things to work together [as a plan] for good for those who love God, to those who are called according to His plan and purpose."*

I went to the studio the next day, and Julie and her team were fantastic. The love of God flowed from them to me with words of compassion. I began to cry. Debbie McNeely, one of the show's co-hosts, began to pray for me and speak The Word of God over me. Still a little nervous, but now feeling empowered by the Holy Spirit to raise up past my fears, I kept repeating in my head: *"I can do all things through Christ who strengthens me."* (Philippians 4:13, NKJV)

I sat on set, took a deep breath, and began telling my story and answering the ladies' questions. A strange thing happened. The more I shared my story, the more I felt FREE! The shackles began to fall off me! The scripture, Revelation 12:11 (KJV), began to breathe new life in me: *"And they overcame him by the blood of the Lamb, and by the word of their testimony; and they loved not their lives unto death."*

Revelation 12:11 became alive in ME! Praise God; The devil is a liar! John 8:44 (KJV) says, *"Ye are of your father the devil, and the lusts of your father ye will do. He was a murderer from the beginning and abode not in the truth because there is no truth in him. When he speaketh a lie, he speaketh of his own: for he is a liar and the father of it."*

During the interview, I shared the one thing they do not tell you when you have an abortion. They never tell you that while you think you can leave the abortion clinic and the problem is solved, the bigger problem begins for the rest of your life; you carry that child with you forever with the constant reminder of what could have been. You take them with you every time you see or hold a baby. While I may not have carried the baby for a few weeks, the memory of my child stays with me.

While I know that when I asked Jesus to forgive me He did, the consequence of my actions will, however, be with me forever, and that is how it should be. I will always live with the regret of that choice, and that's ok, because regret is good. It has taught me to stay close to The Lord and lean closer to Him to make the right choices. If I want to remain in that freedom, I must stay in Christ!

1 John 1:9 (KJV), "If we confess our sins, He is faithful and just to forgive us our sins, and to cleanse us from all unrighteousness."

RAISE UP

The Lord forgave me of my sin, but the memory of that sin stays with me like a scar to remind me not to do it again. Dear Lord, I pray for my unborn child. I know my child is with you, and one day I will see them and live with them for eternity. Lord, I pray you tell them how sorry I am and that if I could do it over, I would have faced my consequences and held them in my arms.

My prayer for you as you read my story, and those of our whole team, is that you will know that God is no respecter of persons; what He did for us, he can and will do for you! He will raise you up and help you to become everything He has called you to be!

Romans 2:11-16 (ESV) "For God shows no partiality. For all who have sinned without the law will also perish without the law, and all who have sinned under the law will be judged by the law. For it is not the hearers of the law who are righteous before God, but the doers of the law who will be justified. For when Gentiles, who do not have the law, by nature do what the law requires, they are a law to themselves, even though they do not have the law. They show that the work of the law is written on their hearts, while their conscience also bears witness, and their conflicting thoughts accuse or even excuse them on that day when, according to my gospel, God judges the secrets of men by Christ Jesus."

Please know that the enemy is a liar and that you have done nothing that the blood of Jesus cannot forgive! Ephesians 1:7 (ESV) *In him we have redemption through his blood, the forgiveness of sins, in accordance with the riches of God's grace.* That means you too! I genuinely feel like some of you reading this book are feeling how I felt. You have made mistakes you regret; you do not feel worthy of Christ's forgiveness. You have believed the lies of the enemy that you are too dirty for God to use you. That is a lie from the enemy. The truth is that we are all sinners who need a savior. Romans 3:23 (ESV) "*…for all have sinned and fall short of the glory of God."*

Romans 3:10-12 (NIV), As it is written: "There is no one righteous, not even one; there is no one who understands; there is no one who seeks God. All have turned away, they have together become worthless; there is no one who does good, not even one."

We are all covered in filthy rags till we receive forgiveness through grace, and The Lord does not remember our transgressions!

Psalm 103:12 (KJV), "As far as the east is from the west, So far hath he removed our transgressions from us."

It is finished once you have repented to Jesus and asked Him into your heart! Then the next step must happen: walking it out. This is a term I learned from Sara Prather, our She Will Conference Prayer Director. If that term is new to you, it means walking out your healing God's way, through prayer, reading and obeying God's word, doing what The Lord says to do and praising Him all the way. The Lord will raise you up and you will overcome!

"I say then: Walk in the Spirit, and you shall not fulfill the lust of the flesh." (Galatians 5:16, NKJV)

When we do this, we will learn to walk in victory. It may not be easy initially, but it will get easier through leaning in and listening to The Holy Spirit.

"And I will ask the Father, and he will give you another advocate to help you and be with you forever—the Spirit of truth. The world cannot accept him, because it neither sees him nor knows him. But you know him, for he lives with you and will be in you. (John 14:16-17, NIV)

I wish I could say I never failed The Lord again after my abortion, but I cannot. I know there must be times when God shakes his head at me. Let's go back, Shortly after my abortion, I met another older man. We got married and were married for seven years. The best thing from that marriage was the birth of my first son, Parker. After seven years of marriage, my husband left me for a younger woman. I fell into a dark place. I was mad at God and began to spiral. I went back to familiar patterns, looking for love in all the wrong places again. I was dating two guys, and somehow, I thought not entirely giving my heart to anyone would protect me from getting hurt, but instead, I felt worse than I have ever felt in my life; I felt dirty. As a believer, you will be miserable when you backslide, and I mean miserable! I had hit rock bottom. I began to

RAISE UP

pray for The Lord to help me escape my mess again, and He did... just not how I had imagined.

I was driving limousines at the time. I had picked up an elegant client - she seemed to have it all together. I drove her to a business meeting in Green Hills. While waiting for her to come out of her meeting, the thought hit me, "I am late". Not late to pick her up, but late as in 'late'. I ran over to Walgreens and bought a test. I went to the bathroom and took the test immediately. My jaw dropped to the floor when the stick turned blue. I thought, "how am I here again?" I know how; I could not believe I was this stupid. I was not a child anymore, I was a grown woman, 25 years old. The blood drained from my body as I sat there thinking about the fallout. Here I was, finding myself pregnant again and this time, I had the added bonus of not one, but two different men that could be the father of my unborn child. I know what you're thinking, "classy", right? I felt like an episode of Jerry Springer in the making.

I got the call to go pick up my client. When I got her in the Limo, I told her that I just found out that I was expecting. She did not know me or my story. She had no idea if I was married, but without skipping a beat, she asked, "are you going to keep it?" It was as if my baby were leftovers in the fridge! I knew I would keep my child, there was no other option this time, but who was she to suggest otherwise? Something rose up in me, and I said "YES, of course, I am". I will never forget her strange look of disappointment (it was very creepy). I was a mother now and knew that my child was not just a mass of tissue but a human life that, if given a choice, would say yes to their life!

The road ahead was not easy, to say the least, but it was one I knew I would face this time, no matter what would happen or how bad the fallout would be. I had to face it no matter what: I had to tell both men and everyone else in my personal life. It was awful to say the least, every bit of it, but not living with the secret was worth it ALL!

When I was eight months pregnant, my ex-husband sued me for custody of my first son, calling me unfit. Shortly after the birth of my second son, Briggs, we went to court. While I might have been a mess in the dating department, I was a good mother. The Lord had blessed me with an excellent job and a stable home for my child. The judge ruled in my favor, but the whole experience shredded me to my core. Had it not been for Jesus and His loving hand using this to guide me back, raising me out of the pit once again, I don't know where I would be. Jesus left the 99 to come for the one, and I was that 1. Praise God!

Matthew 18:12 (KJV), "How think ye? If a man have a hundred sheep and one of them be gone astray, doth he not leave the ninety and nine, and goeth into the mountains and seeketh that which is gone astray?"

     Twenty-six years later, my life looks completely different; While I am imperfect today, I live fully surrendered to my Lord and Savior, Jesus Christ! I found my identity in Him and Him alone. He has taught me to quit falling into the pit. He has taught me to raise up a standard and live a life worthy of His sacrifice! I have learned to take each thought captive and to live a life of victory through my troubles. I have peace that while that young girl who fell into the traps of the enemy is now forgiven for her sins through the blood of The Lamb, my remaining spiritual limp is a beautiful reminder to always lean into Him and not to my own understanding. I know He is always with me and has proven He will never forsake me.

Hebrews 13:5 (KJV), "Let your manner of living be without covetousness, and be content with such things as ye have. For He hath said, "I will never leave thee, nor forsake thee;"

     I am so thankful that The Lord does not throw us away when we fail Him. I love that He can turn our mess into a message. When I began to live my life in line with The Lord's Kingdom principles, everything came into line for me. Not a perfect life, but a life of victory and freedom! That "Better than you ever dreamed" life is what I have today. I remarried an incredible, Godly man named Barry Steelman. My Sister, Tracey, and her husband, John, set us up, and we married nine weeks later. We each had two sons and we were determined to blend our family God's way, loving them as if they were ours biologically together. We have leaned into Proverbs 22:6, knowing that we had to raise them in a Godly home.

"Train up a child in the way he should go; even when he is old he will not depart from it." (Proverbs 22:6, ESV)

RAISE UP

It was not an easy task. The boys often pit Barry and me against one another, causing unneeded conflict. There were some tough years, but we kept our eyes on Jesus. We kept our family in the church and tried not to treat them differently. We don't step on the ones we love. We are all a 'bonus' to each other (if it needs to be differentiated) - Bonus Mom, Bonus Dad, & Bonus Sons. The only time that happens is in respecting our boy's biological parents. Blending a family is not easy; I honestly believe it takes more of Jesus in your life than a traditional family because of all the extra people and the baggage that follows suit. It is not just about the family in your marriage and home; it is the added factor of the exes. You can control what happens in your home, but you cannot control what happens in theirs. If they are not walking uprightly with The Lord, that will also have a ripple effect on you. You must stay prayed up, having your home built on the rock, and be mindful of the shifting sands of the others at play.

Matthew 7:24-27 (KJV), "Therefore whosoever heareth these sayings of mine, and doeth them, I will liken him unto a wise man, which built his house upon a rock: and the rain descended, and the floods came, and the winds blew, and beat upon that house; and it fell not: for it was founded upon a rock. And every one that heareth these sayings of mine, and doeth them not, shall be likened unto a foolish man, which built his house upon the sand: and the rain descended, and the floods came, and the winds blew, and beat upon that house; and it fell: and great was the fall of it."

John 13:35 (NIV), "By this everyone will know that you are my disciples, if you love one another."

Jesus was rejected more than any of us, so who am I to complain? I was blessed when The Lord brought this incredible man to love me, share my life, and help me raise my boys God's way. It is not easy for him either, so we press on and know that hurting people - hurt people (Joyce Meyer) and that we must be the light of Christ to them. Even today, as a Bonus GMommy, you try to love these incredible little GBabies without playing favorites, and BAM, you are reminded that you are not their real grandparent - not by the babies, but others at play. So we continue to press on, knowing that God's LOVE will conquer ALL!

1 Corinthians 13:7-8 (ESV) *"Love bears all things, believes all things, hopes all things, endures all things. Love never ends. As for prophecies, they will pass away; as for tongues, they will cease; as for knowledge, they will pass away."*

Part of raising a standard is teaching others what it looks like to do it God's way. I am determined to leave a legacy that honors my Lord and Savior.

Barry and I are celebrating 25 years of marriage this year; we did it! We blended a family God's way and God will use us to train the next generation to not fall into the pits the enemy sets for them. The mistakes I made earlier in my life sent me on a detour, but The Lord is redeeming that time with a double fold recompense for the time the enemy has stolen from my life and ministry!

Isaiah 61:7 (NIV), *"Instead of your shame you will receive a double portion, and instead of disgrace you will rejoice in your inheritance. And so you will inherit a double portion in your land, and everlasting joy will be yours."*

Revelation 12:11 (KJV), *"And they overcame him by the blood of the Lamb, and by the word of their testimony; and they loved not their lives unto the death."*

Reflecting back, I can see the Lord's hand on my life, leading me and preparing me every step of the way. Before I was ever invited to sit at tables filled with people living out the same calling I have, The Lord has had me serving the people at the table. Long before The Lord had me singing or ministering on a platform, the Lord had me serving them as a photographer for the event. The blessing for me has been the knowledge I have gained from being called to it and learning from others while helping those already ministering.

You can learn a lot by being invisible in the room. You are guaranteed to see the good, the bad, and the ugly while serving them, but it will teach you so many invaluable life lessons.

Serving leaders before leading has empowered me so much to overcome my fears and learn how to treat others by watching behind the scenes. Know this: If you wish to minister effectively, you must honor

RAISE UP

God in your private and personal life first and always. To truly make an impact, your life must mirror what you sing or minister from the platform. Please don't dismiss it when you are asked to help or serve before you live out your calling publicly. He is preparing you for unexpected things so you will be empowered to manage the situations. So, take a breath and grow where you are planted - in time, He will replant you in a bigger pot! You do not want to be re-planted in a bigger pot, or promoted, till you are ready. Know this: He is faithful and His timing is perfect! So, if God is calling you to something and you get the opportunity to serve someone doing that same thing, be humble and do it. Serve with all your heart, doing it as unto God. In time, He will promote you.

*"**Therefore humble yourselves under the mighty hand of God, that He may exalt you at the proper time." (Peter 5:6, NASB)***

I leave you with this, remember you can do ALL THINGS through Christ who strengthens you! The Lord does hold us all in the palm of his hand, just like the song says, and you can trust Him to take care of you! If you allow Him, Jesus will RAISE YOU UP, and you can be a mighty warrior living according to His standards!

In Christ Love, Victoria

VICTORIA STEELMAN

Reflect and Write Your Story
A Journey From Single To Blended Family

Reflect:

In what way does the personal story you've just read connect with your own experiences? Is there common ground between you and the author? Explore the emotions you felt while reading. Where do those feelings stem from and how are they connected to your personal story?

RAISE UP

Writing Prompt:

Reflect on a situation where adversity or negativity was intended to harm you, but through divine intervention, it was transformed for your benefit. Describe how this experience impacted your faith, shaped your character, and influenced your mindset. Explore the lessons learned and the broader perspective gained from witnessing God's ability to turn a negative situation into a positive outcome.

Scripture Connection:

Looking back, can you see where God was in this part of your story? Do any scriptures come to mind?

Chapter Eleven
Sara Prather

Sara's Survival:
Confronting Abuse And Reclaiming Life

My journey to Jesus is one that was never meant to be. Born into a family that took me to church Sunday mornings, Sunday nights, and Wednesday nights, one might think, "what do you mean?" I was meant to know Jesus because my Father in Heaven is a good, good Father, and He ordained it to be. He knew me before I was ever born. He called me for such a time as this. He knew exactly what family I'd be born to, and He knew all that I would endure and overcome. He loved me, and He rescued me. I give God all the glory for who I am today. I am an overcomer by the blood of the lamb, and the word of my testimony! This is my story…

My dad preached at church, was very involved and there was nothing more important than being in that building when we were supposed to be. The church affiliation we were involved in was throughout the United States and we'd come together each summer, usually for church camp in the mountains. From the outside looking in, maybe we looked like a normal, average family. I can't say. I can only speak to what I lived through. I was abused by the church - sexually, physically, mentally, and emotionally - but it was all done in darkness.

For many years I had very little memory before 8 years of age. I always knew something bad had happened but didn't know what. What I knew was that I was an 8-year-old who would have panic attacks regularly. Such bad ones that I'd be taken to the emergency room with thoughts of a heart attack. I was diagnosed with anxiety and put on medication. My home life was also dysfunctional, with lots of physical and emotional abuse. I learned early on to do my best not to be seen or heard. I tried to do everything to perfection, to stay out of the limelight, and I was great at running and hiding out until, hopefully, the smoke cleared. These are all mechanisms I took into adulthood.

At the age of 14, I was raped, but I wasn't a virgin and I didn't know why I wasn't. I had been at a place I wasn't supposed to be, and I had been drinking. Telling anyone was not the thing to do in my mind. I also had someone close to me, laughing, saying that I wanted it. That didn't help either. I spiraled from this point, making one bad decision after another. I had no worth and no trust of anyone. I didn't love Jesus. All I knew was a very angry God and I wanted nothing to do with that. Praise God, He didn't feel the same way about the very messed up girl that I was.

I got pregnant my senior year of high school and married the child's father. We went on to have two more children in our years of marriage and I absolutely adore my children. The marriage was two young people, both with issues, and no way of knowing how to deal with adulthood, marriage, and family. That marriage failed miserably but before it did, I had begun going to church with a childhood friend of mine and her dad. I eventually felt led to get re-baptized and I did so with my dad's guidance through his affiliated church. After I was baptized, I remember being told a series of things that I was now mandated to do. I knew what I was hearing wasn't right, but I didn't know what "right" was.

Once the marriage to my children's father ended, I enrolled my children in counseling to help them through the fall of our household, but when the counselor began to focus on me, I shut it down. I couldn't face my issues. Instead, I continued trying to keep my head above water, taking care of my children and just doing what I believed was right in my own eyes.

Within six months, I met the man who would be my second husband. When my children were at their dad's for the weekend, I liked to frequent a little bar with my friends. It was where I got attention and then would ignore phone calls until those I received attention from would give up. But one night I ran into the guy that became my second husband. There was an instant connection, and he was persistent. He didn't give up, therefore I called it, "God running us straight into each other." If I could put a slap-face emoji right here, I would! There were plenty of red flags, but do you think I was paying attention? At one point, with the mess his life was in, I was headed to the city to rescue him when

SARA PRATHER

I saw a sign at the local church that read, "Do you hear Me now? Signed… God," I responded, "Yes, God, I hear You!!!" Then I continued in the rescue with the eventual marriage taking place.

My kids loved this man: my boys being 8 and 7, and my daughter 2 when he came into the picture. We had a decent life and became part of a community, running a business, and doing all things a normal mid-class family would do. It was at this time that we began going to a little bible church of mostly retired folks. I spent the next five years with God, going line by line, precept upon precept, into the bible. God began showing me through His word, what the Bible actually says compared to what I was taught. Those five years were a vital time in my life!

After this, I began coaching at a ministry-based gym, but that happened slowly. I was taught from a young age that I wasn't allowed to speak, teach, or pray out loud because I am a female. The coach would literally leave me to pray to where I was on the spot and had no choice. This gym helped me find my voice in more ways than one! I began to give a little devotional every class I coached, as was the custom of a coach there, and I would pray before and after each class. Iron sharpening iron is how I would describe that time in my life.

I was growing in my faith and learning more and more each day, all with my husband's blessing. By this time we had moved churches because we felt we needed to plug-in closer to our community. I was staunch that I wasn't going to go to any church with a denominational name on it. I also wanted no part of the politics of the church or to get involved. I simply wanted to love Jesus. I had so much church hurt from my childhood.

During this time my daughter was playing year-round softball with a travel team and most Wednesdays and Sundays were spent on the field. I asked a question during a bible study one night and the pastor said to me, "Your daughter knows softball, but does she know Jesus?" You could tell by the look on his face that he was shocked that came out of his mouth and yet, it was the exact fire I needed to do something. I began to purpose myself of bringing Jesus to the softball fields. This was the next phase in ministry and growth for me.

I was doing strength and conditioning with the team and I began leading devotionals, and prayers with them as well. Eventually, I began to volunteer with The Fellowship of Christian Athletes and was leading

RAISE UP

devotionals with several teams within the organization. As I grew closer to God and continued to walk through the doors that were opening to me, the further my husband spiraled the other way. As I prayed, God impressed upon me that He wanted us both, so I began to battle.

I had just watched War Room, with Priscilla Shirer, and I was going to war in my house. God was teaching me about my authority and spiritual warfare, and I began casting out all that was plaguing my family. After doing this, we had about a month of peace before my husband became horribly worse than before. I didn't understand and began crying out to God. He took me to Luke 11:24-26 (NLT), *"When an evil spirit leaves a person, it goes into the desert, searching for rest. But when it finds none, it says, 'I will return to the person I came from.' So it returns and finds that its former home is all swept and in order. Then the spirit finds seven other spirits more evil than itself, and they all enter the person and live there. And so that person is worse off than before."*

I was so angry and was asking God why He didn't show me this before. I heard in a small, still voice, "I didn't ask you to do this daughter." I have learned as I've grown that walking in the authority of Jesus Christ and all that He has given us, is a walk in relationship with the Holy Spirit who tells us what our Father wants us to know. John 14:26 (NLT) says, *"But the Helper will teach you everything and cause you to remember all that I told you. The Helper is the Holy Spirit that the Father will send in my name."* Things always go better when I'm walking under the direction of the Spirit of Truth.

God quickly rescued my family as the darkness all came to light with my second husband. Overnight, my whole world changed as I discovered the darkness my husband had spiraled into. That darkness landed him in prison for 30 years for his acts against our family. I had three days before warrants were put out for his arrest and a protective order was in place. I thought I needed to know why and when I asked him why, his response was, "All I can tell you is, I started taking those steroids and listening to music that, although the words may not have been satanic, the bands were. I thought I was strong enough to withstand it all but I wasn't." This is what I wrote in my journal a couple of months after this response while journaling about it: "Even now, as I see this shell of a man, who has been and is now so willing to hurt us, I know it is not flesh and blood that I, through God flowing in me, am fighting. Even through the pain and the tears, I will rise. God will see all this through. To the glory of Him who created me, He will take care of me and my family. This I know to be true, in Jesus name."

That declaration was written on August 13, 2017, and I can say today, that God is faithful. He has redeemed me, loved me, and cared for me, and my family, with the care of a Father who looks at us with adoration in His eye. For the next two years, my sons, daughter, and I walked through a grueling time awaiting trial, while my ex-husband received slaps on his hand for violations of bond restrictions and protective orders. God told me not to run. This was the first time I stood and did not run. I stood for my daughter, who was 15 and looked to me on how to handle these grievous violations against her. You see, right before her 15th birthday, she learned the man she called dad was a pedophile. She endured that for six months and under the protection of the FCA camp, spoke about what was happening to her. She is incredibly brave and is a hero in my eyes.

This was the moment I drew a line in the sand. I had questions not of this world and I needed answers not of this world. I called a counselor, whom I refer to as the "good doctor." As my spiritual father/covering would say, when people needed someone with "certificates on the wall, he called the good doctor." Those two were a dynamic duo like I had never seen before and have not seen since. They helped save my life and I am forever grateful. When I sat down with the good doctor, one of the questions I had was, "How did I go from such a bad first marriage and enter into one that fell worse than the first?" The good doctor's response, "I believe you can walk into a room with 100 men, and the one with familiar spirits will be drawn to you, and you to him." Just as Romans 8:16 (ESV) says, *"The Spirit Himself bears witness with our spirit that we are children of God,"* and children of God recognize this in one another. It's likewise for the kingdom of darkness. You see, everything satan does is a direct mimic of the Kingdom of God. satan hasn't created anything new. he (I refuse to give him even the reverence of a capital letter) is a false "god" who built his own kingdom out of jealousy of the one true God. Essentially, Tommy (the good doctor) was telling me I needed deliverance.

RAISE UP

I want to point out that at this point, I had given my heart to Jesus. I had gone deep with Him and was learning the deeper things as I began to pray, seek, ask, and live in communion with Christ. But doing all of this didn't remove the icky that had plagued me my whole life. I needed help and Tommy, along with Curtis Bankston, who I refer to as a spiritual father to me on this earth, walked with me in ways no one else had before. I wanted freedom so much that I was willing to lay it all on the table. I've learned that "laying it all on the table" is a constant as God continues to root up within a surrendered vessel what does not serve Him. Praise God, He is loving and gentle about it! I learned how to come against spirits that don't match the Spirit of God. I could also see them, and God was teaching me how to wield my sword and stand in the authority that He has given me as His daughter. Because I had been so abused my entire life, there were open doors that gave satan legal access through that trauma. Then as I grew, I began to do things that opened doors to the enemy by my own doing. I had to deal with those, first through repentance of my sins, and then through forgiveness.

I remember Tommy looking at me and saying to me, "If you are not willing to forgive, then we need to stop here before we move on." Tommy knew what was still so very fresh for me and my family. He knew what we were facing with my ex-husband and it wasn't out of a lack of compassion that he said this. It was out of compassion for me and my freedom that he said it. He gave me a prayer that I prayed for both ex-husbands and many others. The prayer is this:

"Heavenly Father, from my heart, as an act of my will, not because I feel like it, but because Your word says so, I choose to forgive _____ for _____ (state what you're forgiving the person for). From my heart, I forgive _____ for all of that. I let them go free, I hold nothing to their charge. I release them into Your hands Father, to get vengeance as you so choose. I take all the hurt and anger (resentment, bitterness) out of my heart, I remove it, and place it at the foot of the Cross. I don't want it in my heart, I let it go. And Father, I repent and ask Your forgiveness for having carried it there and I receive Your forgiveness. Holy Spirit, I ask that You fill those places in my heart where that stuff was with Your peace, Your love, and Your joy. In Jesus name, Amen."

I began here and I repeated this prayer often. One day, Curtis and I were at lunch, and he asked me to look at someone. I turned to look and it was a man, whose nasty demons were staring back at me. I could see them and I became angry that Curtis made me look at that. Curtis said, "I want you to see what it looks like, so you won't allow those "familiar spirits" to come back into your life". Curtis then commented on my reaction, and I (angrily) said, "I've said the words of forgiveness, but God has to change my heart!" Curtis whistled and left it alone.

I write this smiling because, as I think back on it, those two men loved me when I was most unlovable. They stood even when I would become angry and lash out. They never backed down and they never turned their back on me. I first learned to trust my Heavenly Father and then I began to learn to trust man. Those angry words I spoke did come to pass. God did change my heart. Only He could do it and He did. If you want to walk in the freedom that Jesus offered you on the Cross, then forgiveness is the first step. It is significant that Jesus went to the cross for the very ones who put Him there. Then one of His last things to say as fully human on this earth was, *"Father forgive them, they know not what they do."* (Luke 23:34, ESV)

God asks us to forgive so that we can be forgiven. (Matthew 6:14-15) As I worked through this, God was leading me on a journey. No more was He allowing me to use the defense mechanisms I had so intricately built up to "protect" myself from the world. I wasn't allowed to run anymore. I couldn't wall myself off and isolate, though God gave me space when I needed it and people to love me when I needed it. God is a God of order, and there is a time for everything under the Son. God started helping me tear down these walls that I had built up over my life. I came to learn that these very walls didn't just separate me from having true, intimate, Godly relationships with people, but they also put a barrier up between me and Him. I was given homework to find a place to, *"Be still and know He is God."* (Psalm 46:10, ESV) I had a beautiful little sanctuary that God had given my family while we walked through the trial we were facing, but that wasn't the place. I would inevitably think of something that needed to be done there. God led me to a cemetery that had water, ducks, wind chimes, and a giant cross. No one bothered me there and people are allowed to grieve there. I had a lot of grief to deal

RAISE UP

with. Then I was asked to picture myself crawling in my Father's lap. That took some time.

I remember sitting there one day, having gone to the wedding of my son's friend. I sat there alone, with my family so broken, watching these two youngsters making vows to one another. It was beautiful and I was so broken. I went to my place after and sat with the Lord. The Spirit of the Lord came, like a soft wind, the chimes lightly sounding off, and a blanket of love wrapped around me. I received a hug, and love like I had never experienced before. I will never forget it. When scripture says that *"He is close to the brokenhearted, those who are crushed in spirit,"* (Psalm 34:18, ESV) He means it. The question is, will we make space to receive it from Him?

I went to Walmart on my way home that night and the Spirit of the Lord was still very much with me. I passed by a mother and a son who looked to be about 12 or so. I heard a screech that was not from this world, and I turned to see and it was the son. The mother was trying to comfort him. I continued on but ended up passing them again. This time it was a direct encounter and the boy screeched again, except it was the demon that had him bound screeching. It came out of him and at me like gnashing of teeth. I felt a barrier of protection about me, and I kept walking. The boy began crying. This boy was bound up with fingers mangled, and I'm sure the world diagnosed him with disabilities, but I encountered the real culprit. I ended up crossing paths with them a third time. This time the mother was trying to direct him away from me, rightfully so, since he was having such severe reactions to me. In the worldly, it looked like a boy reacting to a random woman. In the spiritual, it was the Spirit of God so strong on me that it was causing the demon that had the boy gripped to react. When I encountered them the third time I smiled at the mother and with the boy's mangled fingers, the demon threw up a peace sign at me.

I want to address something here. Just as God and angels are very real, so are satan and demons. It is clear throughout scripture that this is the case. We are in a war, and we have been since the beginning of time. One-third of Jesus' ministry was casting out demons and Jesus gave us a commandment before He went to the right hand of His Father. That commandment is, *"Go into all the world and proclaim the gospel to* the whole creation. Whoever believes and is baptized will be saved, but whoever does not believe will be condemned. And these signs will accompany those who believe; they will speak in new tongues; they will pick up serpents with their hands; and if they drink any deadly poison, it will not hurt them; they will lay their hands on the sick, and they will recover." (Mark 16:15-18, ESV) I'm here to tell you, from studying the Word, being a missionary for Christ, and yielding to His Spirit, that Jesus meant what He said. As Proverbs 30:5 (ESV) says, *"Every word of God proves true; He is a shield to those who take refuge in Him."* I don't want to add or take away from His word. I'm simply sharing my journey with you. God has walked with me every step as I swim in deep waters. His word is truth, and I believe Him. I have encountered much darkness before this and after, and all God is asking me to do is abide in Him.

    That night, I was so exhausted and all I wanted to do was lounge out with a bowl of popcorn, a glass of wine, and watch mindless television. The Lord had already put it on me to stop the glass of wine at night but I was fighting it, and that night I had a terrible attack in the night. Pinned down to my bed, fighting to get the name of Jesus out, I could feel the weight of the demon on me. I was eventually able to get Jesus' name out and cast it out of the room. You see, I was being disobedient. God had asked me to lay down the wine and I didn't. That's what happens when we are out of alignment with God. He'll tell us what to do, and it's to bless us, not to harm us. When we don't, we are telling God, "Don't worry, God, I've got this." And God is a gentleman. He lets us have it.

    The next morning, I dumped the rest of that nice Texan wine right down the drain. It wasn't about drinking in general; it was about me using that as a comfort rather than going to my Father. God wants there to be nothing between His children and Him. He is my comfort and my solace, and when I go to other means to gain that, He'll let me. I've learned to talk to God about everything. He cares about even the smallest details of our lives and He wants to be invited into our days with us. Later, after gaining more healing, I was questioning God about alcohol, since it can be such a debate in the Christian world. He led me to this scripture, *"All things are lawful for me,"* but not all things are helpful. All things are lawful for me, but I will not be dominated by *anything."* (1 Corinthians 6:12 ESV) I was using wine in a way that was dominating me. Food can be just as big of a vice. Or Netflix, and yes, I'm going to say it, even church, or ministry. Sometimes we use these things to keep us busy so that we don't have to sit with God and work through what He wants us to work through. That is placing something in front of Him, even when it's called good by the world, it becomes an idol and puts a wedge between you and Christ.

One day I was going for a run and went to plop my earbuds in with Christian music. All good things to do but God knew I needed to talk to Him. He told me to take my earbuds out and I did. He said, "Talk to me." I told Him I didn't know what to say but then I began pouring my heart out. Yes, God through His Spirit, talks to us. He is our friend, our advocate, and an everlasting help in times of trouble. He gives to us what is given to Him by our Father. If you haven't heard His voice, go on a journey in God's Word about hearing Him, then sit with Him, and tell Him you are listening. Odds are you have heard Him before, and you just didn't understand that it was Him speaking to you. As I poured my heart out, God listened, loved, and comforted me. And I had something to give Him. The burden I was carrying was His, not mine. Many times, God would ask me, "Who am I, Sara?" My response would be different each time. And then He would ask me, "Who are you, Sara?" One time my response was, "I'm a warrior." And God gently said, "No, you are My daughter, My princess." I'm His princess. Selah (chew on that a second) So are you. He loves you. He created you while you were still in your mother's womb. He knows every hair on your head, and He created each one. You are His masterpiece. Beautifully and wonderfully made.

My journey has not been easy. Memories began to come back to me that I had been missing. God is so gracious to us that when you have been through extreme trauma, your brain will fracture off to hold the trauma so that you can continue to function on the surface. That's by God's design. This is called disassociation in the psychology world and there are many forms of disassociation. As I continued this healing journey, I have had memories come back to me that explain what happened to me as a child. God has been faithful in walking with me through everything that surfaces. I have had confirmations given to me to help me understand and I have gained more and more healing as I continue to *"press on toward the goal for the prize of the upward call of God in Christ Jesus."* (Philippians 3:14 ESV) I think John Eldredge states it best in his book Waking the Dead (is there something for me to do here?), "The story of your life is the story of the long and brutal assault on your heart by the one who knows what you could be and fears it."

The things that happened to me over my life aren't what God intended for me. I remember asking Him where He was in the memories I have of being abused. He showed me He was right there with me. He took the pain for me. He carried me through. I should be dead today, given many events in my life, but I am not. That was by God's design that I lived, and that I tell my story. Today, because of what I went through in the past, I have been able to stand in the gap for those who have gone through extreme torture at the hands of evil. They were never meant to do anything but serve the kingdom of darkness, according to what evil people meant for them. But God has other plans and God wins. As Joseph declared to his brothers in Genesis 50:20 ESV, *"As for you, you meant evil against me, but God meant it for good, to bring it about that many people should be kept alive, as they are today."* Joseph's brothers sold him as a slave and told their father he was dead. God made Joseph a ruler that would save many people including the very ones who meant evil against him.

Children are being trafficked every day. I was one of those. There is an underbelly of darkness that no one likes to talk about and, should one of us manage to make it in this world and speak up, it's meant to sound so unbelievable that no one will hear us. I have sat with many who tell their stories of abuse that would make a grown man weep. I have told my own and noticed it's hard for it to even compute in someone's mind. There are evil people out there and they are right under your noses. Children are being sold, raped, used in satanic rituals, and fractured in their minds on purpose, to be so broken that no one will ever believe the atrocities they've been through. Who will love them? Who will advocate for them? Someone chose to love me and advocate for me. I am an overcomer by the blood of the Lamb and the word of my testimony.

God has been faithful in revealing all darkness, and as darkness comes to light, God's cleansing hand is right there to take it all. He has been faithful to hold me, love me, cleanse me, and redeem me. Today,

RAISE UP

even as I continue walking out this journey of healing, I've gotten to witness mighty miracles of God for myself and many others. He never ceases to amaze me!

    God has opened doors too big for me to open and He has closed doors too big for me to close. God has moved mountains in my life and that of my family. Today, I am married to a wonderful man of God. God did that. My agreement with God was, "God if I can serve you better single, let that be so. If I can serve you better married, let that be so, but You are going to have to tell him and me because I'm not doing this without You!" God honored that agreement, and He did tell him and me. We got to court and marry in the most beautiful, Godly manner with our mentors and close friends at our sides. God is faithful! God had given me a word after my second marriage failed. That word was "I will replace all that the locusts have eaten." I took that word home to my daughter and her response was, "Even a dad, mom? Even a dad?" At the time that threw me for a loop. That required something of me, but in 2020 my daughter stood with me as I married the man God so clearly ordained for me, in a sunrise wedding. I am so thankful I get to experience this, this side of heaven. Marriage is the closest intimacy we can have with our Creator while here on this earth. It's a straight depiction of the genuine love of our Father through two people, His son and daughter, not perfect, but deeply loved. And that is what we are, deeply loved.

    I want to end by addressing the one reading this who has been through trauma in her life. I want you to know that you are seen, by your Heavenly Father who created you and by us. We are your sisters and you are loved. You have a safe place to fall with us and, though we are merely people and we can't love you better than our Father whose love is always best, I want you to know you are not alone. Today is your day to rise up. Whatever secrets you've carried it's time to bring them to light. No more can the enemy play with our past, our present, or our future. Today is the day we stand, battle flags posted as a banner of the Lord, and we shout VICTORY! If you need someone to talk to, go to our website and reach out to us. We will be your battle buddy!

    To the one reading this that the Lord has been pressing you to step out of your comfort zone and do something that seems too big for you. Praise God! I just want to say sister, be afraid if you must, but do it!!!! God carries you in His right hand and you have a role to play for His Kingdom. Get to it!

Let me not presume everyone who reads this has given their heart to Jesus. This is the first step. Jesus is a gentleman. He stands at the door knocking but it's up to you to invite Him in. Will you?

Jesus is the healer, the redeemer, our Savior. There are many counterfeit saviors in this world but He is the only one who died and rose again, and He is coming back for His people. Today, if you want to ask Him in your heart, repeat these words, "Jesus, I come before you today and I give my heart to you. My whole heart. All that I am, I surrender to You this very minute. I ask you Jesus to forgive me for all my sins. Wash me clean and make me of you. Have Your way in my life from this day forward. I surrender all of me to you. Cleanse me and make me new, in Jesus name."

If you prayed this prayer, will you reach out to us so we can celebrate with you and walk with you as you continue this journey? We're so thankful for you and are so proud to call you a sister in Christ!

Let me end with a prayer for you, my sister. I pray the Holy Spirit's anointing upon you. That a new fire, Holy Spirit fire, will be stirred up in your heart and that you will move forward in ways that you've never moved before. I pray that God goes before you cutting back all the weeds so that you get to walk right through. That you would not veer to the right nor the left, but have eyes wholly fixed upon Jesus. I pray for a fresh anointing upon you, God's oil poured out upon you, that every step you take will be anointed. That you would move when Holy Spirit says move, and speak when He says speak, and be still and quiet otherwise. God, I ask You to encamp Your angels about my sister, to stand guard over her and her household, and that You open doors too big for her to open and close doors too big for her to close. Her feet planted upon the rock that she shall not be shaken. I declare she will live, and she will not die, and she will declare the works of the Lord forever more! In Jesus name I pray, amen.

RAISE UP

Raise up your flag as a banner my sister!!!! Psalm 60:4 (ESV) says, *"You have set up a banner for those who fear you, that they may flee to it from the bow."* Banners served as battle flags in ancient wars. Today we raise our flags together and recover all that the enemy has stolen from us! Will She Raise Up? SHE WILL!!!!!

SARA PRATHER

Reflect and Write Your Story
Confronting Abuse And Reclaiming Life

Reflect:

In what way does the personal story you've just read connect with your own experiences? Is there common ground between you and the author? Explore the emotions you felt while reading. Where do those feelings stem from and how are they connected to your personal story?

RAISE UP

Writing Prompt:

Reflect on instances where you have extended forgiveness to others and received it in return. Explore the emotions and transformations that took place during these experiences. Delve into the concepts of grace and mercy, describing how they played a role in your ability to forgive and be forgiven. Share the impact of these acts on your relationships, personal growth, and understanding of compassion.

SARA PRATHER

Scripture Connection:

Looking back, can you see where God was in this part of your story? Do any scriptures come to mind?

Chapter Twelve
Shelsea Becker

SHELSEA BECKER

Shelsea's Exodus:
Escaping Egypt's Hold And Finding Freedom

    I will share my personal journey of how God's divine intervention brought me out of a place of darkness and despair, and guided me towards a life filled with hope, purpose, and light. With the use of paint, a canvas, and the guidance of the Holy Spirit, I discovered the transformative power of deliverance and the unwavering love of God. Join me as I recount the remarkable moments that shaped my spiritual awakening and led me on a path of redemption.

    Sitting in my counselor's office, my gaze drifting into the distance, I listened to him speak about the importance of releasing what was buried deep inside. The desire for freedom burned within me, yet I resisted his request. For three long weeks, we faced off like adversaries in an old western showdown, unyielding in our positions. However, I knew that something had to give for healing to take place. Frustrated, I wondered if there was another way, questioning my own resistance to his simple request: journaling.

    At the time, I couldn't explain why the mere mention of writing halted me in my tracks. "Shelsea, you need to find a way to express those emotions, thoughts, hurts, and pains," he insisted. And I reluctantly replied, "Fine, but I won't write!"

    There I sat, trapped in a state of pain and fear, longing for freedom but paralyzed by my own resistance. I found myself at a dead end. As I stared aimlessly, the Holy Spirit granted me a vision. I saw a room enveloped in canvas, all four walls and the ceiling covered. In the center of that room stood me, surrounded by buckets of paint—each one a different color: red, green, blue, and yellow. As I observed the scene, I witnessed myself plunging my hand into a pail, grasping a handful of paint, and forcefully slinging it onto the wall. This process was repeated

RAISE UP

with various colors—slinging, throwing, screaming, and crying. Each throw brought forth a verbal and spiritual release, encapsulating the intense emotions within me. Paint splattered everywhere, much like the havoc my hurt wreaked in real life. It was a stark realization: hurt people hurt people.

Suddenly, I comprehended what my counselor had been trying to convey. Snapping back to reality, I looked at him and asked, "Can I paint?" After a brief pause, he nodded, and we decided to give it a try.

In that moment, God was paving a way for me when neither of us could see a path forward. I desperately needed an escape from the internal battle consuming me. Looking back, painting offered a safer outlet for expressing my turmoil compared to writing. Eventually, I discovered the reason behind my resistance to writing or journaling. I feared facing the thoughts I had about myself, the labels that defined me, and the emotions I had so skillfully concealed. What if someone read what I wrote? What would they think of me? Am I losing my sanity? Did these things truly happen to me, or am I exaggerating?

Have you ever grappled with these questions? One specific question initiated the unraveling of the tangled web that ensnared me: "How did I end up here?" Perhaps you've whispered that same inquiry under your breath.

Armed with the counselor's approval and the Holy Spirit's vision, I eagerly embraced the opportunity to paint. My precious mother made space for me in her garage. She hung up a painter's drop cloth measuring 8'x 8' as my canvas, and took the kids out on an errand. I gathered all the painting supplies I could find and turned on some soft worship music.

Staring at the blank canvas was overwhelming. I couldn't throw the paint inside the garage. So there I was staring at it. What now? At that moment, I turned to prayer. "Lord, I don't know what to do. What should I paint?" A persistent answer echoed within me: "Paint a cross." However, I resisted. Painting a cross seemed too common, too ordinary. But the message persisted: "Paint a cross."

Remembering the scripture that says His grace is sufficient, I realized I had tested it firsthand. Recognizing that God was speaking to me, I understood that I should obey His command. Still, I wondered why I resisted.

SHELSEA BECKER

But he said to me, "My grace is sufficient for you, for my power is made perfect in weakness." Therefore I will boast all the more gladly about my weaknesses, so that Christ's power may rest on me. (2 Cor 12:9, NIV)

Taking a paintbrush and dipping it into brown acrylic, I started shaping the cross on the canvas. The vertical beam measured about 18 inches in length and the horizontal beam was approximately 15 inches in width. I felt content with what I had created and expected approval to follow.

Yet, instead of praise, I received a question: "Is that how big you think I am?" I saw the bigger picture. The cross I had painted was so small compared to the expansive canvas. Did I truly believe that the God of Angel Armies was smaller than my problems?

"The LORD of Heaven's Armies is here among us;
The God of Israel is our fortress.
Come, see the glorious works of the LORD:
See how he brings destruction upon the world.
He causes wars to end throughout the earth.
He breaks the bow and snaps the spear;
He burns the shields with fire.
"Be still, and know that I am God!
I will be honored by every nation.
I will be honored throughout the world."
The LORD of Heaven's Armies is here among us;
The God of Israel is our fortress."
(Psalm 46:7-11, NLT)

Though my human words failed me, I continued praying, now in the Spirit. When we don't know what to pray, the Spirit intercedes on our behalf with unspoken groanings. Seeking further guidance, I returned to the canvas, switched brushes, and expanded the cross. Its arms stretched out, and then I heard a tender voice explaining His vastness: "I AM as far as the east is from the west."

"In the same way, the Spirit helps us in our weakness. We do not know what we ought to pray for, but the Spirit himself intercedes for us through wordless groans." (Romans 8:26, NIV)

RAISE UP

God replied to Moses, "I Am Who I Am . Say this to the people of Israel: I Am has sent me to you." (Exodus 3:14, NLT)

*"For as high as the heavens are above the earth,
so great is his love for those who fear him;
as far as the east is from the west,
so far has he removed our transgressions from us.
As a father has compassion on his children,
so the Lord has compassion on those who fear him; "
(Psalm 103:11-13, NIV)*

With the cross now four feet tall, I refined the edges and tidied up my strokes, feeling satisfied with my painting. Yet, I knew painting for the sake of it wasn't my purpose here. Another question emerged from the Lord: "Don't you know there is no end to me?" "I AM the Alpha and Omega; the beginning and the end."

"I am the Alpha and the Omega, the First and the Last, the Beginning and the End." (Rev 22:13, NIV)

At that moment, I was acutely aware of the presence of the Creator of the universe in the room with me. Tears streamed down my face, blurring my view of the canvas as I softened the hard edges I had just painted. I couldn't confine God within boundaries. The cross continued to grow on the canvas.

I am praying.
I am painting.
He is present.

Under the powerful influence of the Holy Spirit, I found myself compelled to paint a thorny crown delicately resting on top of the cross. In that artistic gesture, I wholeheartedly recognized Jesus as my King, my Lord. It was a profound realization that when we truly understand His lordship, we willingly surrender every aspect of our lives.

"For in Christ all the fullness of the Deity lives in bodily form, and in Christ you have been brought to fullness. He is the head over every power and authority." (Colossians 2:10, NIV)

As I immersed myself in this act of surrender, I took a paintbrush and splattered the canvas with vibrant red, symbolizing the precious blood that was shed for my sake. The weight of His presence intensified, evoking a flood of tears that cascaded down my face. In that moment, I felt a profound sense of intoxication, as if being consumed by the overwhelming depth of His love and sacrifice. It was a divine encounter that left me humbled and transformed.

"For God was pleased to have all his fullness dwell in him, and through him to reconcile to himself all things, whether things on earth or things in heaven, by making peace through his blood, shed on the cross." (Colossians 1:19-20, NIV)

Praying and painting, I stood there, fully surrendered to His leading, no longer resisting. Then I heard Him say, "Write." Unlike before, I didn't resist. I knew I was safe in the hands of the Maker. The words He asked me to write held me captive, carrying immense pain and emotion. I had been burdened by them for so long. Under each arm of the cross, I wrote a list of words that had become strongholds in my life—"ugly," "used," "abused," "betrayed." After creating the lists, I prayed over each word, releasing its grip on me, wiping it away with the red paint symbolizing the blood of Christ. With each release, I felt lighter, and each stronghold crumbled. It was a time of deliverance. I was being set free.

"For though we live in the world, we do not wage war as the world does. The weapons we fight with are not the weapons of the world. On the contrary, they have divine power to demolish strongholds. We demolish arguments and every pretension that sets itself up against the knowledge of God, and we take captive every thought to make it obedient to Christ." (2 Cor 10:3-5, NIV)

Isaiah 61:3 (NIV) came to mind: *"To provide for those who grieve in Zion— to bestow on them a crown of beauty instead of ashes, the oil of joy instead of mourning, and a garment of praise instead of a spirit of despair. They will be called oaks of righteousness, a planting of the LORD for the display of his splendor."* This encounter with God lasted 45 minutes. The One who placed the stars in the sky and commands the sea, entered the room with me. Instead of me questioning Him, He questioned me. What did I believe to be true? Who did I think He was? It was reminiscent of Peter's experience when Jesus asked him, "Who do you say I am?"

"Where were you when I laid the earth's foundation?
Tell me, if you understand.
Who marked off its dimensions? Surely you know!
Who stretched a measuring line across it?
On what were its footings set,
or who laid its cornerstone—
while the morning stars sang together
and all the angels a shouted for joy?
"Who shut up the sea behind doors
when it burst forth from the womb,
when I made the clouds its garment
and wrapped it in thick darkness,
when I fixed limits for it
and set its doors and bars in place,
when I said, 'This far you may come and no farther;
here is where your proud waves halt?'"
(Job 38:4-11, NIV)

"When Jesus came to the region of Caesarea Philippi, he asked his disciples, "Who do people say the Son of Man is?" They replied, "Some say John the Baptist; others say Elijah; and still others, Jeremiah or one of the prophets." "But what about you?" he asked. "Who do you say I am?" Simon Peter answered, "You are the Messiah, the Son of the living God." (Matthew, 16:13-16)

There was a divine purpose behind God's request for me to paint a cross. It all starts at the cross. I must go to the cross to receive what Christ did for me; salvation and deliverance. Jesus didn't just die for my salvation, but also so that I can experience freedom while here on earth.

"For the message of the cross is foolishness to those who are perishing, but to us who are being saved it is the power of God."
(1 Cor 1:18, NIV)

In Christ, we experience true deliverance, and we no longer have to walk as dead men. Instead, we can walk in the fullness of life and freedom that He offers. He came to give us life and to give it abundantly.

"I have come that they may have life, and have it to the full." (John 10:10, NIV)

"Deliverance" has often been misunderstood or portrayed in a negative light, but in its essence, it means being set free. Jesus paid the ultimate price to ransom us and provide deliverance. In Him, we find freedom from sin, which is also known as salvation. We all need a Savior, a Rescuer, to free us from the chains that bind us.

"But Christ has rescued us from the curse pronounced by the law. When he was hung on the cross, he took upon himself the curse for our wrongdoing." (Galatians 3:13, NLT)

When we go through challenging times, we might find ourselves in the valley of the shadow of death. However, the key is to keep moving forward and not camp there indefinitely. Do not set up camp in the valley of the shadow of death. Psalm 23 says to walk through the valley. We should acknowledge and feel the emotions but not get stuck in despair. I tell others "Feel the feels, but don't live there."

If you feel trapped or caged, you might be experiencing spiritual bondage, and in such cases, you need spiritual deliverance. The One to call upon for rescue is the ultimate Rescuer, Jesus Christ. Through Him, strongholds can be broken, and we can be set free from the bondage that holds us captive, just like a prisoner awaiting liberation.

Beyond salvation, Jesus continues to deliver us from spiritual strongholds. His love, sacrifice, and grace have the power to break the chains that bind us to sin, fear, and other spiritual bondages. As we surrender our lives to Him and invite Him into our hearts, His transformative presence works to set us free from the strongholds that once held us captive. With His help, we can overcome any obstacle, find healing from past wounds, and experience true freedom in every aspect of our lives. His deliverance is ongoing, extending to every area of our being, bringing hope, restoration, and a renewed sense of purpose.

RAISE UP

"May the God of hope fill you with all joy and peace as you trust in him, so that you may overflow with hope by the power of the Holy Spirit." (Romans 15:13, NIV)

    Before this experience of spiritual deliverance, I had experienced a true physical deliverance. An exodus to be exact.
    I always found it puzzling how the Israelites would constantly whine, complain, and express a longing to return to Egypt, despite God's miraculous deliverance from the hands of Pharaoh during the exodus. (I highly recommend reading the book of Exodus.) His power was evident in their freeing from slavery, making their desire to go back seem incomprehensible.
    Then after experiencing a life-changing event, my perspective altered entirely. I finally understood how the Israelites felt during those moments of uncertainty and doubt. Like them, I encountered a situation that shifted my understanding and empathy for their struggles.
    Sitting on the guest room bed in my mother's house, a few weeks before the painting encounter that freed me from spiritual bondage, I found myself earnestly pleading to God for guidance. I had been separated from my husband for what felt like 40 days, facing a critical decision. Should I leave for good or return? The weight of knowing God's displeasure towards divorce and the judgment from the church weighed heavily on me. I was torn within myself, battling conflicting emotions.
    In search of direction, I turned to the book of Exodus, hoping to find wisdom in the Israelites' deliverance story. As I read, a profound revelation struck me. In my spirit, I heard a clear question, "Do you want to return to Egypt?" The answer resounded from deep within, a resolute "NO!" This immediate response brought clarity to my heart, guiding my next steps. I then heard God's tender voice affirming, "I have already delivered you, do you want to go back?" Again, my answer was a firm "NO!" I knew in my soul that I had been set free. I had taken myself and my children out of the oppressive and binding circumstances. Why would I willingly return to that state of oppression and bondage?
    The intimate way in which God spoke to me left no room for doubt. I knew with absolute certainty what I needed to do. I knew in my knower, you know? With courage and conviction, I moved forward with the divorce, knowing it was the path to true freedom and a brighter future

for myself and my children. (I do not recommend divorce. You must hear from God for yourself for your situation.)

Even after experiencing God's undeniable deliverance, fear, uncertainty, and discomfort can still take hold when faced with the unknown. The Israelites' journey through the wilderness was not easy, and they had to learn to trust in God's provision and guidance.

Similarly, in our own lives, we may experience times of deliverance and liberation, but that doesn't mean we won't face difficulties afterward. Challenges might arise, and we could be tempted to doubt or look back to what was familiar, even if it wasn't ideal. It's a reminder that our faith journey involves ongoing trust in God, especially during times of transition or uncertainty. Through it all, God remains faithful, leading us towards a promised land of His provision and blessings if we continue to follow Him with faith and obedience.

"Consider it pure joy, my brothers and sisters, whenever you face trials of many kinds, because you know that the testing of your faith produces perseverance. Let perseverance finish its work so that you may be mature and complete, not lacking anything."
(James 1:3,4 NIV)

It's truly a testament to God's faithfulness that He has led me to a land of abundance and blessings, akin to the promised land flowing with milk and honey. In that land, I found a knight in shining armor—a remarkable individual who fought for me, protected me, and wholeheartedly supported me and the children.

"God will do this, for he is faithful to do what he says, and he has invited you into partnership with his Son, Jesus Christ our Lord."
(1 Corinthians 1:9, NLT)

James has been a constant source of strength, love, and encouragement, standing by our side through thick and thin. His unwavering support has been a tangible representation of God's love. James recognized the calling on my life before I did. It is because of his great faith that I am in ministry today.

Experiencing deliverance, both physically and spiritually, has left a permanent mark on my life. The profound transformation I underwent has made me unrecognizable compared to my former self. The old burdens and chains have been discarded, replaced by a newfound sense of freedom and renewal.

Physically, the deliverance I encountered brought about significant changes in my life circumstances, liberating me from oppressive situations and allowing me to step into a brighter future. Spiritually, the impact has been equally profound. The weight of guilt, fear, and insecurities has lifted, making way for a deep sense of peace and contentment. I am free to run through the field of flowers and chase after the things of God. This has put my feet on a pathway to lead a team of incredible leaders in ministry. I now embrace my Christ-filled life with a fresh perspective, leaving behind the limitations that once held me back. I live a life of adventure now. I no longer live to survive, but now I live to experience all that the Lord has for me. There was a time I could not even think about tomorrow as I was so concerned with staying above the fray on a day to day basis. I can now dream. This journey of deliverance has allowed me to shed the old habits, beliefs, and mindsets that hindered my growth. I walk in the knowledge that I am loved, valued, and redeemed.

With gratitude, I embrace the newness that has emerged from this deliverance. I am a living testimony to the power of God's grace and the transformation that can occur when we surrender our lives to Him. I am no longer bound by the past; instead, I confidently step into the future, knowing that I am a new creation, equipped to live a life of purpose and significance.

"But we all, with unveiled face, beholding as in a mirror the glory of the Lord, are being transformed into the same image from glory to glory, just as by the Spirit of the Lord." (2 Corinthians 3:18, NKJV)

One of the most profound lessons I've learned through this journey of deliverance is the discovery of my true identity in Jesus. Previously, I felt lost and unsure of who I was and my purpose in life. Seeking validation from others, I looked to human approval for direction, which only left me feeling empty. However, through this process of deliverance, I've come to understand that my identity is rooted in being a child of the Most High God. He has a unique plan and purpose for my life, fearfully and wonderfully crafting me to preach, teach, and reach others. Embracing this truth, I no longer seek man's approval or guidance for my path. Instead, I turn to God, His Word, and the guidance of the Holy Spirit to lead and direct me.

"For you are all children of God through faith in Christ Jesus." (Galatians 3:26, NLT)

"For I know the plans I have for you," declares the Lord, "plans to prosper you and not to harm you, plans to give you hope and a future." (Jeremiah 29:11, NIV)

"I praise you because I am fearfully and wonderfully made; your works are wonderful, I know that full well." (Psalm 139:14, NIV)

Knowing who I am in Christ has given me a newfound sense of confidence and assurance. I walk in the knowledge that I am loved, accepted, and chosen by God. His grace empowers me to step into the calling He has placed on my life, bringing me fulfillment and a sense of purpose that I had never experienced before. My journey of deliverance has led me to embrace my true identity, and I now live with a deep trust in God's leading and a firm reliance on His unfailing guidance.

Feeling unworthy of the calling was an initial struggle for me. It took time to move the knowledge of God's purpose for me from my head to my heart. I devoted long hours to seeking the Lord, engaging in deep conversations with Him, and wrestling with scripture. Understanding that I was called to take up my cross daily and follow in the footsteps of Jesus, as described in Isaiah 61 became a pivotal turning point in my life.

"The Spirit of the Sovereign Lord is on me,
because the Lord has anointed me
to proclaim good news to the poor.
He has sent me to bind up the brokenhearted,
to proclaim freedom for the captives
and release from darkness for the prisoners, a
to proclaim the year of the Lord's favor
and the day of vengeance of our God,
to comfort all who mourn,
and provide for those who grieve in Zion—

RAISE UP

to bestow on them a crown of beauty
instead of ashes,
the oil of joy
instead of mourning,
and a garment of praise
instead of a spirit of despair.
They will be called oaks of righteousness,
a planting of the Lord
for the display of his splendor.
They will rebuild the ancient ruins
and restore the places long devastated;
they will renew the ruined cities
that have been devastated for generations.
Strangers will shepherd your flocks;
foreigners will work your fields and vineyards.
And you will be called priests of the Lord,
you will be named ministers of our God.
You will feed on the wealth of nations,
and in their riches you will boast.
Instead of your shame
you will receive a double portion,
and instead of disgrace
you will rejoice in your inheritance.
And so you will inherit a double portion in your land,
and everlasting joy will be yours.
"For I, the Lord, love justice;
I hate robbery and wrongdoing.
In my faithfulness I will reward my people
and make an everlasting covenant with them.
Their descendants will be known among the nations
and their offspring among the peoples.
All who see them will acknowledge
that they are a people the Lord has blessed."
I delight greatly in the Lord;
my soul rejoices in my God.
For he has clothed me with garments of salvation
and arrayed me in a robe of his righteousness,
as a bridegroom adorns his head like a priest,
and as a bride adorns herself with her jewels.
For as the soil makes the sprout come up

SHELSEA BECKER

and a garden causes seeds to grow,
so the Sovereign Lord will make righteousness
and praise spring up before all nations."
(Isaiah 61, NIV)

These verses from Isaiah resonated with my soul, as they spoke of God's anointing and commissioning to bring good news to the humble and afflicted, bind up the brokenhearted, and proclaim release to those held captive—both physically and spiritually. They were a reminder that I am called to be an instrument of His grace and love, sharing the message of freedom and redemption with those in need.

Through this process of wrestling with scripture and spending time with the Lord, I gained a deeper understanding of His heart for the broken, the oppressed, and the mournful. My purpose became clearer—to comfort those in distress and provide solace to those who grieve. It was a journey of internal transformation, as I allowed God's truth to shape my identity and empower me to fulfill His calling.

As I embraced the weight of this divine commission, I found the courage to step into the path God had prepared for me. I may still face challenges and uncertainties, but knowing that I am walking in His anointing and guidance fills me with a sense of purpose and peace. It is a continual process of surrendering to His leading and trusting in His unfailing grace, knowing that He equips and empowers me to carry out His mission in the lives of others.

This is just a part of my story. I could share with you the profound impact of burying three important women in my life: my firstborn, my mother, and my grandmother, in that order. However, that part of my testimony will have to wait for another day. In this snippet of my life that I've shared, I encountered the Rescuer, the Deliverer, and the Lover of my soul, who calls me worthy, righteous, and redeemed. How about you? How do you know God? Have you experienced His presence and movement in your life?

RAISE UP

Reflect and Write Your Story
Escaping Egypt's Hold And Finding Freedom

Reflect:

In what way does the personal story you've just read connect with your own experiences? Is there common ground between you and the author? Explore the emotions you felt while reading. Where do those feelings stem from and how are they connected to your personal story?

SHELSEA BECKER

Writing Prompt:
Paint a vivid picture of your current life circumstances and surroundings. Describe the emotions and sensations that accompany the realization of being an overcomer. Reflect on the journey that brought you to this point and explore how your perspective has evolved. Share the lessons learned and the sense of accomplishment that comes with overcoming challenges.

RAISE UP

Scripture Connection:

Looking back, can you see where God was in this part of your story? Do any scriptures come to mind?

Write Your Story

As you reach the culmination of this creative journey, take a moment to appreciate how your narrative has unfolded through the prompts you've followed. With each word you write, your story gains depth and significance. Your RAISE UP story is one that resonates with the depth of your experiences. As you prepare to finalize your composition, remember that your submission signifies not just consent, but a courageous act of sharing.

Your vulnerability is not just acknowledged, but deeply respected and valued. It's through sharing the depths of our journeys that we not only inspire, but also connect on a profound level. Your story has the potential to transcend its pages, becoming a beacon of hope and encouragement for those who encounter it. By offering your experiences with authenticity, you contribute to a narrative that can bridge gaps and foster understanding.

Incorporating Jesus into every area of your story adds a layer of depth and insight that can take healing to a new level. Seeing where He was in the midst of the situation brings life to the dark places. Sharing the ways in which your journey has intersected with your faith can provide peace, guidance, and a sense of purpose to others who may be navigating similar paths. As you walk deeply with Jesus, your story becomes a testament to His transformative power and unwavering love.

Remember, your narrative is not just a chronicle of challenges, but a testament to triumph. By sharing how you've overcome obstacles through your faith, you become an embodiment of the concept of being an overcomer. Your story, touched by grace, carries the potential to inspire others to embrace their faith and find strength in their struggles.

As your story finds its way into the hearts of those who read it, know that you are contributing to a mosaic of human experiences. Each story shared adds richness and depth to the collective tapestry of lives. Your willingness to share invites others to do the same, fostering an environment where healing, understanding, and faith can flourish. This is how we build community in a very authentic, real way.

Thank you for choosing to share your story with us. Your bravery and your faith shine brightly through your words, touching lives and inspiring others to embrace their own stories of triumph.

Please share your RAISE UP story at: yourstory@lynministries.org

-Shelsea

About the Authors

Heather Grissom

Heather is a She Will Conference Worship Leader as well as being a musician and songwriter. She is a wife of 17 years to her highschool sweetheart and has 3 beautiful children. She serves the faithful King in the local church with her husband, who is the pastor. In her free time, Heather loves to travel and do absolutely anything outdoors with her family.

Christy Catlin

Christy is a She Will Conference Worship Leader. She is also a pastor, worship leader and author and has been serving in ministry with her husband for the last 20 years. They have 4 children that keep their lives full of laughter and chaos. Their life goal is to see the church rise up in Holy Spirit power and experience genuine freedom & unity.

Kelly Levatino

Kelly is a Bible teacher, one of the She Will Conference Speakers and the National Marketing Director. She is a proud wife to Elian and mother to Lexi and Allie. In her free time, Kelly enjoys drinking coffee, watching UGA football and not cooking.

Liz Catlin

Liz is one of the She Will Conference Speakers and the National Hospitality Director. She is also a writer, radio/podcast host and co-leader with her husband for The Launch Ministry. She refers to herself as the "Wife of a godly husband, Mom to Kingdom builders and Granny to world changers."

Bev McCann

Bev is a singer/songwriter and one of the She Will Conference Speakers. She has been married to the love of her life for over 30 years, is a mother to 4 children and grandmother to 17. She is also owner of a Christian media company called Nashville 37201 TV. She loves to sing, laugh, cook, golf and travel, but most of all she loves to share Jesus everywhere she goes.

Laura Anne Smith

Laura Anne is the She Will Conference National Registration Director. She and her husband of thirty-two years homeschooled their two sons, who are now grown, and spent 8 years helping children with Bible memory at a national level. She continues now as a homeschool tutor on an individual basis and works with TN early intervention services.

Thresa Lawson

Thresa is one of the She Will Conference Speakers and the National Hello Hard Director. She is a doctoral prepared nurse practitioner and ordained minister and is often described as a fiery bundle of energy. Thresa is the mother of four children and grandmother of fourteen. In her spare time, she enjoys gardening and working on her ranch in Mount Calm, TX, where she lives with her husband.

Tammy Manning

Tammy is one of the She Will Conference Speakers and the National Outreach Director. She is also an encourager and connector. She has served the local church in ministry for 24+ years. Tammy is a wife, mother, grandmother and lover of Jesus and tentmaker for the Kingdom of God.

Jessica Cornelison

Jessica is the She Will Conference National A/V Director. She has served in ministry for 20 years as Children's Church Director, A/V Director and Women's Ministry Leader. She spent 6 years as a missionary teacher in Africa and China and currently serves as Administrative Assistant to three different ministries. In her free time, outside of taking a nap, Jessica enjoys playing piano/guitar, reading and practicing assorted yarn crafts such as crocheting, knitting, embroidery and cross-stitch.

Victoria Steelman

Victoria is one of the She Will Conference Speakers and the National Development Director. She is also a Christian Country Recording Artist, songwriter and the She Will Worship Director. Victoria is a wife, mother and GMommy to 9 grandchildren.

Sara Prather

Sara is one of the She Will Conference Speakers and the National Prayer Director. She is also a prayer intercessor, minister of the Gospel and missionary for Christ. Sara is a wife, mother to three amazing children, mother-in-law to two beautiful women and "Eema" to five grandchildren. She is a student of Christ who strives to serve as the Holy Spirit directs and considers home to be where the Lord sends her.

Shelsea Becker

Shelsea is the President of LYN Ministries, INC. and the founder of She Will Conference. She is a speaker, humorist, radio personality and creator of Girl's Weekend God's Way. Her best friend and greatest supporter is her husband, James, and she has two children, Savanna and Bryce. Shelsea enjoys her hot tub, sunrises over the ocean and telling everyone about the love of Jesus.

To book any of our speakers for your event please visit https://www.lynministries.org/booking

Made in the USA
Columbia, SC
21 February 2024